THE GREAT MINNESOTA HOT DISH

Theresa Millang

ADVENTURE PUBLICATIONS
Cambridge, Minnesota

A special thank you to all who contributed to this cookbook.

Copyright 1999 by Theresa N. Millang
Published by Adventure Publications, Inc.
820 Cleveland St. S.
Cambridge, Minnesota 55008
1-800-678-7006
All Rights Reserved
ISBN 1-885061-25-0
Book and Cover Design by Jonathan Norberg
Eighth Printing

TABLE OF CONTENTS

INTRODUCTION

When I moved to Minnesota, I found three things that are unique to Minnesota. Minnesota weather...beautiful in the summer; great for skiing in the winter. Minnesota Nice...a quality I learned to admire very early on. Minnesota Hot Dish...casserole to most other folks in the nation. This cookbook is an ode to Minnesota Hot Dish.

A Hot Dish is a combination of one or more ingredients, including, meat, fish, fowl, noodles, rice, grains, with a sauce and bits of vegetables to give it texture and color, all put together into one baking dish, be it glass, porcelain, iron, ceramic, etc., and placed in the oven to be brought out as one complete meal. Here in Minnesota there are hot dishes meant to be served for different occasions. There's the "Company" hot dish, this would be of a more elegant presentation, such as seafood (not tuna). The "Baby Shower" hot dish, this could be tuna. Then there's the hot dish you serve at "Funerals," this one depends on the area. The "Neighbor is Sick" hot dish, this would be ground beef and macaroni in tomato sauce. There's the "Potluck" hot dish, this one could be a bean or corn side dish hot dish. There's the "Brunch" hot dish, eggs of course, and perhaps a bubbly, fruit cobbler dessert hot dish. You are expected to serve bread and maybe a salad with hot dish.

It is said the French created the first hot dish, oops, casserole. This cookbook has recipes dating back to the early 1900s, some from my husband's Scandinavian mother's recipe collection, a time when some recipes did not include can size, cooking time, or oven temperature, etc., and on to the 1950s, a time when canned soup came full force into the market, a boon to the homemaker. This was an easy way to prepare a Hot Dish, tuna being a favorite. As the years marched on, Minnesota, a heavily Scandinavian populated state, began to incorporate other foods in new Hot Dishes. Tex-Mex became very popular. Then came Cajun, Creole, Tofu, Southern, and more Chinese hot dishes. The possibilities are endless.

Today's hot dishes are using a lot of the same ingredients, but in different combinations. There are many new fresh ingredients on the market, and many convenient canned sauces and seasoning packets one can use in preparing a quick delicious meal. One great advantage of hot dish is you can prepare most of them in advance, refrigerate or freeze them until ready to put in the oven, and have a full meal to enjoy without having to tend to it until you are ready to pull it out.

The hot dish recipes in this cookbook include Chicken and Turkey, Beef, Pork, Seafood, Eggs, Side Dishes and Desserts. I hope you will enjoy this collection of classic, ethnic, and yes, some gourmet recipes.

CHICKEN and TURKEY

Anne's Chicken and Rice

- 1 6-ounce package seasoned long grain and wild rice, uncooked
- 2 tablespoons corn oil
- 6 meaty, skinless chicken thighs, lightly seasoned with salt and ground black pepper
- 1/2 cup chopped onions
- 1/2 cup sliced celery
- 1 4.5-ounce jar whole mushrooms, drained
- 1 10 3/4-ounce can condensed cream of chicken soup, mixed with 2 cups cold water

PREHEAT OVEN TO 350°F

Spread rice into a lightly greased 13x9x2-inch baking dish. Sprinkle evenly with seasoning mix in packet. In a saucepan, over medium heat, heat corn oil. Add chicken; brown slightly. Remove chicken; place over rice. Add onions to same saucepan; stir and cook 2 minutes. Spoon over chicken. Place sliced celery and mushrooms around chicken. In same saucepan, bring soup mixture to a boil; pour over all. Cover and bake 1 hour. Uncover and bake about 20 minutes or until chicken is done. Serves 6.

Serve this meaty hot dish with a shredded cabbage and carrot salad, tossed with Italian dressing.

Audrey's Chicken-Shrimp

- 2 whole boneless, skinless chicken breast, cut into 8 equal pieces
- 1/2 cup all-purpose flour
- 3 tablespoons butter, divided
- 1 medium onion, thinly sliced
- 1 10-ounce can cream of shrimp soup, undiluted
- 1/2 cup whole milk
- 1 16-ounce can stewed tomatoes
- 1/4 teaspoon dried thyme, crushed
- Pinch dried oregano
- Dash soy sauce
- 1 pound peeled fresh shrimp
- Hot cooked long grain white rice

PREHEAT OVEN TO 375°F

Coat chicken with flour; shake off excess. In a saucepan, over medium heat, melt 2 tablespoons butter. Brown chicken on both sides; remove chicken from saucepan. Add remaining butter to same saucepan. Add onion; stir and cook until tender. Add soup, milk and tomatoes; stir until heated. Add thyme, oregano, soy sauce and shrimp; mix well. Place chicken into a 13x9x2-inch glass baking dish. Pour heated soup-shrimp mixture over chicken. Cover tightly with foil. Bake 45 minutes. Uncover; bake 10 minutes. Serve over hot cooked rice. Serves 8.

This special dish may be prepared a day ahead, refrigerated, and baked the next day. Serve with a green salad and warm rolls...buttered of course.

Baked Beans Rice and Chicken

2 tablespoons corn oil

6 boneless, skinless chicken breast halves, cut into strips, seasoned with salt and black pepper as desired

1 cup uncooked long grain white rice

1/2 cup chopped onions

1/2 cup chopped green bell pepper

2 cloves garlic, chopped

1 teaspoon chili powder

2 cups chicken broth or water

1 14-ounce can stewed tomatoes

1 16-ounce can baked beans

PREHEAT OVEN TO 375°F

In a saucepan, heat oil over medium heat. Add chicken; stir and cook until browned. Set aside. Add rice, onions, bell pepper and garlic in same saucepan; stir and cook 2 minutes. Combine all ingredients into a large bowl; mix well. Spoon mixture into a greased 13x9x2-inch glass baking dish. Cover with foil. Bake 50 minutes or until rice is cooked. Serves 6.

Serve this hot dish with tossed salad along with warm crusty bread.

Bev's Chicken Hot Dish

1 1-year old chicken (not a fryer) boiled, boned and meat cut up, reserving broth

6 tablespoons butter, divided

1 medium size onion, ground

8 cups soft bread crumbs

2 stalks celery finely chopped

2 eggs

1/2 teaspoon salt

1/2 teaspoon sage

Pinch ground black pepper

1/2 tablespoon baking powder

1 1/2 cups whole milk

1 10 3/4-ounce can condensed cream of mushroom soup, undiluted

1 cup reserved chicken broth

PREHEAT OVEN TO 325°F

Place chicken into a 11x7x2-inch glass baking dish. In a small saucepan, melt 5 tablespoons butter. Add onion; stir and cook until browned. Place onion and butter into a large bowl. Add bread crumbs eggs salt, sage, pepper, baking powder and milk; mix well. Spoon over chicken. Sprinkle with 1 tablespoon cut up butter. Top with mushroom soup and chicken broth. Cover and bake 1 1/2 hours. Add more broth if seems too dry during last 30 minutes of baking. Serves 10.

Bev lives in northern Minnesota...a good cook. Her chicken hot dish requires a little time preparing, but is well worth it. Serve with a salad and jellied cranberry sauce along with warm rolls.

Biscuit-Topped Chicken Hot Dish

2 cups cooked cubed chicken

2 10¾-ounce cans condensed cream of chicken soup, undiluted

2 9-ounce packages frozen mixed vegetables, thawed

1 teaspoon grated onion

½ cup whole milk

1 egg, slightly beaten

1 cup boxed biscuit mix

PREHEAT OVEN TO 400°F

In a 2½-quart oval glass baking dish, mix together chicken, soup, vegetables and grated onion. In a bowl, mix together milk, egg and biscuit mix. Pour over chicken mixture. Bake uncovered, about 35 minutes or until bubbly and biscuits are golden. Serves 6.

This hot dish is like a home-made pot pie. A salad will complete the meal.

9

Broccoli Chicken Hot Dish

- 1 bunch fresh broccoli, cooked, drained
- 4 whole chicken breast, boned and precooked
- 2 10¾-ounce cans condensed cream of chicken soup, undiluted
- 3 tablespoons mayonnaise
- 1 tablespoon fresh lemon juice
- ¼ teaspoon curry powder
- 1 cup shredded cheddar cheese
- 5 tablespoons grated Parmesan cheese
- ¼ cup dry bread crumbs

PREHEAT OVEN TO 350°F

Place broccoli on bottom of a 13x9x2-inch baking dish. Top with chicken. In a bowl mix together soup, mayonnaise, lemon juice and curry powder; pour mixture over all. Sprinkle with cheeses and bread crumbs. Bake 30 minutes or until very hot. Serves 8.

Serve this hot dish with salad and buttered rolls.

Cajun-Flavored Chicken 'n Rice

1 large green bell pepper, cut into 1-inch pieces

1¼ cups water

½ cup whole kernel corn, fresh or frozen

1 6-ounce package Spanish rice mix

1 15-ounce can diced tomatoes with garlic, undrained

½ teaspoon each: black pepper, onion powder, garlic powder

¼ teaspoon each: cayenne pepper, paprika, thyme

4 skinless, boneless chicken breast halves

PREHEAT OVEN TO 350°F

In a 3-quart glass lightly greased baking dish, combine bell pepper, water, corn, rice, including seasoning in packet, and tomatoes until well mixed. In a small bowl, mix together seasonings; sprinkle over chicken. Place chicken in baking dish; gently press into rice mixture. Cover and bake about 45 minutes or until rice is tender and chicken is no longer pink. Serves 4.

Serve this hot dish with a crisp green salad.

Cashew Chicken Hot Dish

4 boneless skinless chicken breast halves, cut into cubes

2 tablespoons butter

1 medium size onion, diced

1 10-ounce can sliced mushrooms, drained

1 cup uncooked long grain regular white rice

1 tablespoon chicken bouillon granules, mixed with 1 1/2 cups boiling water

1 teaspoon ground ginger

2 cups broccoli pieces

1 cup cashew nuts

Pinch ground black pepper

1 teaspoon soy sauce, or as desired

Parsley sprigs

PREHEAT OVEN TO 375°F

In a saucepan, over medium heat, stir and cook chicken in butter until done, about 5 minutes; spoon mixture into a 2 1/2-quart round glass baking dish. Add onion, mushrooms, rice, boiling water and ginger; mix well. Cover and bake 30 minutes. Stir in broccoli; bake 10 minutes or until vegetables are done. Remove from oven and let stand a few minutes. Stir in 1/2 cup cashews, pepper and soy sauce. Sprinkle remaining cashews on top. Place under broiler, (without the cover) to brown. Remove from oven. Garnish with parsley. Serves 4.

Serve this hot dish with match-stick fresh cut carrots, an orange-pineapple molded gelatin salad, along with crusty rolls.

Cheddar Chicken 'n Asparagus

1½ pounds fresh asparagus spears, halved, partially cooked, drained

2 tablespoons corn oil

½ teaspoon salt

¼ teaspoon black pepper

4 boneless skinless chicken breast halves

1 10¾-ounce can condensed cream of chicken soup, undiluted

½ cup mayonnaise

1 teaspoon lemon juice

½ teaspoon curry powder

1 cup shredded cheddar cheese

PREHEAT OVEN TO 375°F

Place the asparagus into a greased 9x9-inch square glass baking dish. Heat oil in a saucepan, over medium heat. Season chicken with salt and pepper; brown on both sides in heated corn oil. Place chicken over asparagus. In a bowl, combine soup, mayonnaise, lemon juice and curry powder. Mix well; pour over chicken. Cover and bake 40 to 50 minutes or until chicken is tender and juices run clear. Sprinkle with cheese. Remove from oven. Let stand 5 minutes before serving. Serves 4.

A good luncheon hot dish...serve with an assortment of breads and fresh fruit.

Cheesy Chicken & Pasta

2 tablespoons butter

1/4 cup chopped onions

2 tablespoons all-purpose flour

11/4 cups whole milk

1 16-ounce package frozen creamy cheddar vegetables and pasta

11/2 cups cubed cooked chicken

1/4 cup dry bread crumbs, mixed with 1 tablespoon melted butter

PREHEAT OVEN TO 350°F

Melt butter in a saucepan. Add onions; stir and cook until tender. Gradually stir in flour. Gradually add milk, stirring constantly, until thickened. Stir in frozen vegetables and pasta, and chicken. Pour mixture into a 11/2-quart glass baking dish. Sprinkle top with bread crumb mixture. Bake 35 to 45 minutes or until thoroughly heated. Serves 4.

A quick and easy way to prepare a hot dish. Serve with sliced tomatoes and rolls.

Chicken Alfredo Hot Dish

3 cups cubed cooked chicken

2 cups cooked wild rice

3 green onions, chopped

1 cup sliced fresh mushrooms

1/2 cup chopped green bell pepper

1/4 cup water

Pinch ground black pepper

1 14-ounce can artichoke hearts, drained and quartered

1 10-ounce container refrigerated regular Alfredo sauce

1/2 cup shredded Parmesan cheese

PREHEAT OVEN TO 350°F

In a bowl, combine all ingredients except Parmesan cheese; mix well. Spoon into a greased 2-quart glass baking dish. Top evenly with cheese. Cover and bake about 35 minutes or until hot and bubbly. Serves 4.

This hot dish is easy to put together. Serve with green salad and French bread...buttered of course.

Chicken Artichoke & Rice

- 1 3-pound chicken, cut into serving pieces, skin removed, seasoned lightly with salt and black pepper
- 2 tablespoons corn oil
- 1 medium size onion, chopped
- 3 cloves garlic, chopped
- 1/2 cup uncooked regular long grain white rice
- 1 cup low sodium chicken broth
- 1 teaspoon grated lemon rind
- 1/2 teaspoon fresh lemon juice
- 1 bay leaf
- 1/2 teaspoon dried thyme
- 1/2 teaspoon dried rosemary
- 1 9-ounce package frozen artichoke hearts, cooked and drained

PREHEAT OVEN TO 350°F

In a heavy saucepan, over medium heat, brown chicken in corn oil; remove and set aside. Add onions; stir and cook until tender. Add garlic and rice; stir and cook 2 minutes. Add broth, lemon rind and juice, bay leaf, thyme and rosemary. Bring to a simmer, and cook 2 minutes; discard bay leaf. Spoon mixture into a 4-quart baking dish. Add browned chicken and artichokes, distributing evenly. Cover with foil. Bake about 1 hour or until chicken and rice test done. Serves 4.

A green salad will complete this delicious chicken hot dish.

Chicken-Broccoli Hot Dish

- 1 tablespoon corn oil
- 4 boneless, skinless chicken breast, cut into chunks
- 1 small onion, minced
- 1 14-ounce can chicken broth
- 2 cups elbow macaroni, cooked 5 minutes according to package directions, drained
- 8 ounces process cheese spread, cut up
- 1 10-ounce package frozen chopped broccoli, thawed

PREHEAT OVEN TO 350°F

In a large saucepan heat corn oil. Add chicken and onions; stir and cook until chicken is no longer pink. Stir in broth. Bring to a boil. Stir in macaroni, cheese and broccoli; mix well. Pour mixture into a 2-quart baking dish. Cover and bake until macaroni is tender, about 25 minutes. Serves 6.

Serve this hot dish with a lettuce and tomato salad.

Chicken Cacciatore

1¼ cups uncooked quick-cooking rice

2 tablespoons chopped fresh parsley, divided

1 14½-ounce can chicken broth

1 6-ounce can tomato paste

1 4-ounce can sliced mushrooms, drained

¾ cup water

¼ cup dry white wine or apple juice

1 medium onion, chopped

¼ cup chopped green bell pepper

1¼ teaspoon dried basil

1 teaspoon garlic salt

½ teaspoon Italian seasoning

¼ teaspoon black pepper

6 skinless chicken breast filets

1 cup shredded Mozzarella cheese

¼ cup grated Parmesan cheese

PREHEAT OVEN TO 350°F

Spread rice in bottom of a lightly greased 13x9x2-inch glass baking dish. In a bowl, combine 1 tablespoon parsley and remaining ingredients except chicken and cheeses. Pour over rice. Arrange chicken on top of rice. Cover and bake 50 minutes. Uncover; sprinkle top with Mozzarella and Parmesan cheese. Bake 5 minutes. Sprinkle with remaining parsley just before serving. Serves 6.

Serve this dish with a salad of mixed greens.

Chicken Chow Mein

- 1/2 cup chopped onions
- 2 stalks celery, chopped
- 1/4 cup butter
- 1 10³/4-ounce can condensed cream of mushroom soup, undiluted
- 1/2 cup chicken broth
- 1 tablespoon soy sauce
- 3 cups cubed cooked chicken
- 1/2 cup sliced fresh mushrooms
- 1 3-ounce can chow mein noodles
- 5 tablespoons salted cashew halves

PREHEAT OVEN TO 350°F

In a saucepan, stir and cook onions and celery in butter until tender. Stir in soup, chicken broth and soy sauce. Add chicken and mushrooms; stir and cook until hot. Pour mixture into a greased 2-quart baking dish. Sprinkle with chow mein noodles and cashews. Bake uncovered until bubbly hot, about 25 minutes. Serves 4.

A quick hot dish to prepare...for extra color, add a teaspoon chopped red bell pepper before baking.

Chicken Cordon Bleu

- 4 boneless, skinless chicken breast halves, flattened to 1/4-inch thickness
- 2 teaspoons Dijon-style mustard
- 1/2 cup shredded Swiss cheese
- 1/2 cup finely chopped, fully cooked ham
- 2 tablespoons minced pimientos
- 1 tablespoon minced green pepper
- 1 egg, beaten
- 2 tablespoons cold water
- 5 tablespoons all-purpose flour, mixed with 1/4 teaspoon salt
- 6 tablespoons dry bread crumbs
- Corn oil

PREHEAT OVEN TO 350°F

Spread chicken breast with mustard. In a bowl, mix together cheese, ham, pimientos, and green pepper; place equal portions on center of each breast. Bring one end of breast over mixture. Fold in sides; roll up jelly-roll fashion, pressing ends to seal. In a bowl, mix together egg and water. Place flour and bread crumbs in each a separate bowl. Dip chicken into egg mixture, coat with flour, then dip back into egg mixture, then roll in bread crumbs. Refrigerate 1 hour. In a small heavy skillet heat 1-inch deep corn oil. Fry each roll until browned. Place into an 8-inch square baking dish. Bake 30 minutes or until chicken test done. Serves 4.

Serve this "blue ribbon" dish with rice pilaf and buttered asparagus.

Chicken-Couscous Hot Dish

- 1 6-ounce box couscous with sun-dried tomatoes
- 4 boneless, skinless chicken breast halves, lightly seasoned with salt and black pepper
- 2 cloves garlic, finely chopped
- 1 16-ounce package button mushrooms, halved and lightly sauteed in 1 teaspoon olive oil
- 1¼ cups water
- 1 tablespoon olive oil
- ¼ teaspoon dried basil

PREHEAT OVEN TO 350°F

Spread couscous and tomatoes evenly onto bottom of a lightly greased, 10-inch square baking dish. Place chicken over top. Sprinkle garlic over chicken. Top with mushrooms, including liquid. Pour water over top. Drizzle evenly with olive oil. Sprinkle with basil. Cover and bake 35 to 40 minutes or until chicken test done. Serves 4.

Couscous is a granular form of pasta often used like rice...this dish combines it with chicken, mushrooms and sun-dried tomatoes.

Chicken & Crab Hot Dish

1/4 cup butter

1/2 cup finely chopped onions

1/4 cup all-purpose flour

1 cup chicken stock

1 cup light cream

1/2 teaspoon salt

1/4 teaspoon black pepper

2 cups cooked chicken, cut into large pieces

1 cup cooked peas

1 cup fresh crab meat, picked over

1 cup buttered soft bread crumbs

PREHEAT OVEN TO 350°F

In a saucepan, over medium heat, melt butter. Add onions; stir and cook until tender. Stir in flour until blended. Gradually add stock and cream. Stir in salt and pepper. Bring to a boil; cook, stirring constantly 2 minutes. In a buttered 1 1/2-quart glass baking dish, layer chicken, peas and crab meat. Cover with sauce. Top with bread crumbs. Bake about 30 minutes or until browned on top and is very hot and bubbly. Serves 6.

Chicken and crab meat...serve this hot dish for a special luncheon along with salad and warm rolls.

Chicken Divan For Two

1 cup whole milk

1 3-ounce package cream cheese

1/2 teaspoon Worcestershire sauce, or 1 teaspoon lemon juice

1 cup cooked broccoli florets, drained

1/2 cup shredded sharp cheddar cheese

2 chicken breast, cooked and sliced

1/2 cup soft bread crumbs, mixed with 2 tablespoons melted butter

PREHEAT OVEN TO 350°F

In a saucepan, over low heat, stir milk and cream cheese until smooth. Stir in Worcestershire sauce. Arrange broccoli in bottom of a 10x6-inch baking dish. Layer with shredded cheese, chicken and cream cheese sauce. Top with bread crumbs. Bake 30 to 35 minutes or until very hot. Serves 2.

This hot dish is perfect for that special someone ...serve with a salad and crusty bread.

Chicken and Dumplings

- 6 boneless, skinless chicken breast halves
- 1 medium size onion, chopped
- 2 stalks celery, chopped
- 2 small size carrots, sliced
- 1/2 teaspoon dried sage, crushed
- 1/8 teaspoon dried parsley, crushed
- 1/8 teaspoon ground black pepper
- 2 14-ounce cans low-sodium chicken broth
- 1 cup all-purpose flour
- 2 teaspoons baking powder
- 1/4 teaspoon salt
- 1 tablespoon grated Parmesan cheese
- 1/2 cup whole milk, mixed with 2 tablespoons corn oil

PREHEAT OVEN TO 325°F

Place chicken into a greased 2 1/2-quart glass baking dish. Mix together onion, celery and carrots; spoon mixture over chicken. Sprinkle evenly with sage, parsley and pepper. Pour broth over all. In a bowl, mix together flour, baking powder, salt and Parmesan cheese. Gradually stir in milk mixture. Mix well to form a dough. Form dough into 2-inch balls; drop over top of last layer. Cover tightly. Bake 1 1/2 hours. Serves 6.

Chicken and dumplings...a comfort food!

Chicken Enchiladas

2 cups shredded cooked chicken

1/2 cup chopped onions, cooked in butter until tender

1 1/2 cups shredded Monterey Jack cheese

1/2 cup jarred sliced roasted red bell pepper, or homemade

1 4-ounce can chopped green chilies

1 1/2 cups dairy sour cream, divided

1 10-ounce can enchilada sauce

8 8-inch flour tortillas

1 1/2 cups shredded cheddar cheese

Shredded lettuce

Chopped tomatoes

PREHEAT OVEN TO 375°F

In a bowl, mix together, chicken, onions, Monterey Jack cheese, bell pepper, chilies and 1 cup sour cream. Spread 2 teaspoons enchilada sauce on each tortilla; top each with 1/2 cup chicken mixture. Roll up tortillas and place into a lightly greased 13x9x2-inch glass baking dish seam side down. Top with remaining enchilada sauce. Sprinkle with cheddar cheese. Grease a piece of tin foil, and cover dish, greased side down. Bake about 40 minutes or until thoroughly heated. Remove from oven. Top each with shredded lettuce, tomatoes and remaining sour cream when serving. Serves 8.

For variation, use corn tortillas instead of flour. Heat a small amount of corn oil in a saucepan and fry each corn tortilla 2 seconds on each side.

Chicken Fajita Hot Dish

- 1 8-ounce box red beans and rice
- 1 4-ounce can sliced ripe olives, drained
- 1 4-ounce can diced green chilies drained
- 8 tenderloins of chicken breast, lightly seasoned with ground black pepper
- 2 cups water
- 1 15-ounce can diced tomatoes
- 1 cup shredded Monterey Jack cheese
- 1 cup crushed crushed tortilla chips
- Dairy sour cream

PREHEAT OVEN TO 350°F

Spread red beans and rice (not the seasoning packet) onto bottom of a 13x9x2-inch glass baking dish. Top with olives and chilies, then top with chicken. In a saucepan, bring water to a boil. Add tomatoes and seasoning packet mix; stir. Pour over top of chicken mixture. Cover; bake 45 minutes. Uncover; sprinkle with cheese and tortilla chips. Bake 5 minutes or until chicken test done. Garnish with sour cream, as desired, when serving. Serves 4.

A green salad tossed with a vinegar and oil dressing will compliment this hot dish.

Chicken Hash

4 large potatoes, peeled, boiled in salted water, drained, and mashed with 1/4 cup heavy cream, 2 table-spoons butter, salt and ground black pepper to taste, set aside

4 tablespoons butter

1 cup chopped green onions, white parts only

1/2 cup chopped celery

2 tablespoons all-purpose flour

1 cup chicken broth or stock

3/4 cup heavy cream

3 cups chopped cooked chicken

Salt to taste

Ground black pepper to taste

3/4 teaspoon dried thyme, crumbled

4 eggs

2 teaspoons chopped fresh parsley

PREHEAT OVEN TO 350°F

Melt butter in a large saucepan. Add onions and celery; stir and cook 3 minutes. Gradually stir in flour; stir and cook 3 minutes. Stir in broth and cream. Bring to a boil, stirring constantly. Stir in chicken, salt and pepper to taste and thyme. Pour mixture into a greased, shallow oblong 1 1/2-quart glass baking dish. Spread potatoes over chicken mixture. Make four depressions with back of a large spoon. Bake 15 minutes. Remove from oven. Carefully break eggs into depressions. Season eggs with salt and pepper to taste. Bake about 15 minutes or until eggs are set to desired consistency. Remove from oven. Garnish with chopped parsley, and serve. Serves 4.

For variation, use chopped cooked turkey.

Chicken Hot Dish

5 tablespoons butter

6 tablespoons all-purpose flour

1³/4 cup whole milk

1 cup canned chicken broth

2¹/2 cups cubed cooked chicken

1³/4 cups cooked long grain regular white rice

¹/2 teaspoon salt

Pinch black pepper

¹/3 cup chopped green bell pepper

2 tablespoons minced onion

1 4-ounce can mushroom stem and pieces, drained

¹/3 cup slivered almonds

PREHEAT OVEN TO 350°F

In a large saucepan, over medium heat, melt butter. Gradually stir in flour; stir and cook 1 minute. Add milk and chicken broth. Bring to a boil, stirring constantly; stir and cook 1 minute. Add remaining ingredients; mix well. Spoon mixture into a 2¹/2-quart glass baking dish. Bake uncovered about 45 to 50 minutes, or until very hot and bubbly. Serves 6.

This is a hot dish that's made in minutes. Serve with buttered peas and soft buttered rolls.

Chicken Linguine Hot Dish

2 cups cubed cooked chicken

1 9-ounce package refrigerated linguine, rinsed with hot water, drained

1 10³/₄-ounce can condensed cream of chicken soup, undiluted, heated

1 cup chicken broth, heated

¹/₂ cup finely chopped onions

1 tablespoon fresh chopped parsley

¹/₂ cup diced green bell pepper
Pinch ground black pepper

3 plum tomatoes, cut into wedges

3 tablespoons sliced green onions

¹/₂ cup shredded cheddar cheese

PREHEAT OVEN TO 350°F

In a bowl, combine all ingredients except tomatoes, green onions and shredded cheddar cheese. Spoon mixture into an 8x8x2-inch glass baking dish. Bake uncovered 40 minutes or until thoroughly heated and is bubbly. Top with tomatoes, green onions and shredded cheddar cheese. Bake uncovered until cheese is melted. Serves 6.

Serve with salad and choice of warm, crusty bread.

Chicken Noodle Hot Dish

3³/4 cups wide egg noodles, uncooked

1 10³/4-ounce can condensed cream of chicken soup, undiluted

1³/4 cups whole milk

2 cups chopped cooked chicken

1 10-ounce package frozen chopped broccoli, thawed

1 tablespoon minced yellow onion

1/4 teaspoon garlic powder

6 tablespoons grated Parmesan cheese

1/4 teaspoon ground black pepper

PREHEAT OVEN TO 350°F

Cook noodles according to package directions but less 3 minutes cooking time; drain. In a saucepan, mix together soup and milk; stir and cook until hot. Add remaining ingredients, including noodles; mix. Spoon mixture into a 2-quart baking dish. Cover and bake about 30 minutes or until hot and bubbly. Sprinkle top with additional Parmesan cheese, if desired. Serves 4.

Serve this hot dish with salad and buttered bread.

Chicken Parmigiana

1 16-ounce package thin noodles

4 boneless, skinless chicken breast halves, flattened to 1/4-inch thick

1/4 cup all-purpose flour

1 cup dry bread crumbs

1/2 cup grated Parmesan cheese

2 teaspoons dried Italian seasoning

1/4 teaspoon salt

2 eggs, beaten

6 tablespoons corn oil

1 8-ounce package fresh mushrooms, sliced and sauteed in butter

1 28-ounce jar mushroom spaghetti sauce, heated

3/4 cup shredded Mozzarella cheese

1/4 cup grated Parmesan cheese

PREHEAT OVEN TO 350°F

Cook noodles according to package directions until just tender, but not quite done. Place into a 2-quart glass baking dish. Coat chicken with flour. In a bowl mix together bread crumbs, Parmesan cheese, Italian seasoning and salt. Dip chicken in eggs; coat with crumb mixture. Heat oil in a saucepan; fry each piece of chicken to brown. Place chicken over noodles. Top with mushrooms and spaghetti sauce. Top with Mozzarella cheese. Sprinkle with Parmesan cheese. Bake uncovered 35 minutes or until chicken is done. Serves 4.

Serve with a green salad and warm garlic bread.

Chicken with Peas Hot Dish

- 2 tablespoons corn oil
- 4 skinless, boneless chicken breast halves, seasoned with salt and ground black pepper
- 1 cup chopped onions
- 1 cup regular long grain white rice, uncooked
- 1 medium red bell pepper, coarsely chopped
- 1/4 teaspoon salt
- 1/4 teaspoon ground turmeric
- 1/4 teaspoon crushed red pepper flakes
- 2 cups chicken broth
- 1/2 cup frozen sweet peas, thawed

PREHEAT OVEN TO 350°F

In a saucepan, heat corn oil over medium-high heat. Add chicken; quickly brown on both sides. Remove and set aside. Add chopped onions to same saucepan; stir and cook until tender, but not brown. Add rice, bell pepper and seasonings; stir and cook 1 minute. Stir in chicken broth; bring to a boil. Spoon mixture into a 3-quart baking dish. Place chicken on rice mixture; press down lightly. Cover and bake about 45 minutes or until rice is tender and chicken is no longer pink. Stir in peas the last 10 minutes of cooking time. Fluff rice just before serving. Serves 4.

This is colorful hot dish...very tasty too. Serve with a green salad tossed with an Italian-type dressing.

Chicken Reuben Hot Dish

- 4 whole boneless, skinless chicken breasts, halved
- 1/4 teaspoon salt
  Pinch ground black pepper
- 1 tablespoon butter
- 2 tablespoons chopped onions
- 1 16-ounce can crisp sauerkraut, well drained
- 4 slices natural Swiss cheese
- 1 1/4 cups thousand island salad dressing

PREHEAT OVEN TO 325°F

Place chicken into a greased 13x9x2-inch glass baking dish; sprinkle with salt and black pepper. In a saucepan, heat butter. Add onions; stir and cook until tender. Add sauerkraut; stir and cook 1 minute. Place mixture over chicken. Top with cheese. Pour dressing over cheese. Cover with foil. Bake 1 1/2 hours. Serves 4.

Serve this hot dish with dark rye bread.

Chicken Rice 'n Beans

- 1 cup uncooked regular long grain white rice
- ½ chicken broth
- ½ cup chopped onions, cooked in butter 5 minutes
- 1 16-ounce can hot chili beans in sauce, undrained
- 1 16-ounce can pinto beans, drained
- 1 10-ounce package frozen chopped broccoli, thawed
- 8 slices bacon
- 4 boneless, skinless chicken breast halves, lightly seasoned with salt and ground black pepper
- 1 cup shredded Monterey Jack cheese with jalapeno peppers

PREHEAT OVEN TO 350°F

In a bowl, mix together rice, chicken broth, onions, beans and broccoli. Pour mixture into a shallow 2-quart glass baking dish. Wrap 2 slices of bacon around each chicken half. Place chicken on top of rice mixture. Bake uncovered about 55 minutes or until chicken test done and is no longer pink in middle. Remove from oven. Sprinkle with cheese. Return to oven; bake until cheese is melted. Serves 4.

Serve this hot dish with a crisp green salad.

Chicken Rice-Nut Hot Dish

- 2 tablespoon corn oil
- 4 chicken breast halves, lightly seasoned with salt and ground black pepper
- 1 cup onion, chopped
- 3 large cloves garlic, chopped
- 1 6-ounce package quick-cooking long grain and wild rice with seasoning packet
- 2 cups water, boiling hot
- 1 2-ounce jar diced pimientos, drained, optional
- 6 tablespoons coarsely chopped walnuts

    Chopped fresh parsley

PREHEAT OVEN TO 350°F

In a saucepan, heat corn oil over medium-high heat. Add chicken, onions and garlic; brown chicken well on all sides; remove chicken from pan. Add rice; stir and cook 1 minute. Stir in water. Stir in seasoning packet. Stir in pimientos and nuts. Spoon mixture into a shallow 8-inch square baking dish. Place chicken on rice mixture; press down slightly into rice. Cover and bake about 45 minutes or until rice is tender and chicken is no longer pink. Garnish with parsley when serving. Serves 4.

Serve with a crisp salad, steamed broccoli and favorite bread.

Chicken-Stuffing Hot Dish

1 8-ounce bag onion and sage bread stuffing mix

1/2 cup butter, melted

1 cup water

3 1/2 cups cooked diced chicken

1/2 cup chopped onions

1/2 cup chopped celery

1/2 cup mayonnaise

2 eggs

1 1/2 cups milk

1 10-ounce can condensed cream of mushroom soup, mixed with 1/2 cup whole milk

1 cup grated cheddar cheese

PREHEAT OVEN TO 325°F

In a large bowl, mix together stuffing mix, butter and water; spread half the mixture onto bottom of a lightly greased 13x9x2-inch baking dish. In another bowl, mix together chicken, onions, celery and mayonnaise; spread over stuffing in baking dish. Top with remaining stuffing mixture. In a bowl, beat together eggs and milk; pour over all. Cover with foil and let stand 20 minutes. Spread mushroom soup over top; cover and bake 40 minutes. Sprinkle top with cheese; bake 10 minutes. Serves 10.

You can make this hot dish a day ahead of time; cover and refrigerate overnight. If refrigerated, remove cover, and take out 1 hour before baking.

Chicken Tetrazzini

- 4 tablespoons butter, divided
- 2 cloves garlic, minced
- 5 tablespoons all-purpose flour
- 3 cups chicken broth
- 1/2 cup whipping cream
- 1/2 teaspoon each, salt and pepper
  Pinch ground nutmeg
- 1/2 pound wide egg noodles, cooked in salted water to barely tender
- 1/4 cup minced shallots or onion
- 1/4 cup sliced shiitake mushrooms
- 1/2 pound white mushrooms, sliced
- 1/4 teaspoon dried thyme
- 3 tablespoons dry sherry
- 1 cup frozen peas, thawed, divided
- 3 cups cooked chicken, cut into large chunks
- 1/4 cup grated Parmesan cheese

PREHEAT OVEN TO 450°F

In a saucepan, melt 3 tablespoons butter. Add garlic; stir and cook 30 seconds. Add flour; cook and stir 1 minute. Gradually stir in broth, cream, salt, pepper and nutmeg until blended. Bring to a boil, stirring constantly; remove sauce from heat. Place drained noodles into a bowl. Stir in 1 1/2 cups sauce. In a large saucepan, add remaining butter and shallots; stir and cook 1 minute. Add mushrooms and thyme; cook until tender. Add sherry; boil 1 minute. Layer half the noodles, with 1/2 cup peas into a shallow 2 1/2-quart glass baking dish. Top with half of the chicken then half the mushrooms. Repeat layers. Pour remaining sauce on top. Top with Parmesan cheese. Bake uncovered until hot and bubbly, about 25 minute. Serves 6.

This creamy chicken-pasta hot dish is a snap to prepare with leftover roasted chicken.

Chicken Veggies 'n Rice

- 6 boneless chicken thighs, lightly seasoned with salt and pepper
- 2 tablespoons corn oil
- 2 tablespoon butter
- 1 cup uncooked long grain rice
- 2 cloves garlic, chopped
- 1 1/2 cups tomato vegetable juice
- 1 cup water
- 1 3-ounce can sliced mushrooms
- 1 cup chopped onions
- 1 cup chopped celery
- 1/4 cup sliced black olives
- 1 teaspoon salt
- 1/4 teaspoon black pepper
- 1/2 teaspoon dried marjoram, crushed
  Pinch crushed saffron
- 1 cup frozen peas, thawed
- 1 cup fresh tomatoes wedges

PREHEAT OVEN TO 375°F

In a saucepan, brown chicken in corn oil and butter over medium heat. Remove chicken. Add rice to same saucepan; stir and cook until golden. Add garlic; stir and cook 1 minute. Stir in vegetable juice and water. Add remaining ingredients except peas and tomatoes; mix. Spoon mixture into a 13x9x2-inch glass baking dish. Top with chicken, pressing lightly into mixture. Cover with foil. Bake 1 hour. Remove from oven. Add peas evenly over dish. Top with tomato wedges, seasoned lightly with salt. Cover; return to oven. Bake 20 minutes. Serves 6.

Serve this delicious hot dish, with a crisp lettuce, broccoli and cauliflower salad, tossed with an Italian-type dressing along with hard rolls.

Chicken Wild Rice

- 3/4 cup uncooked wild rice
- 2 tablespoons butter
- 1 medium size onion, chopped
- 2 cloves garlic, finely chopped
- 1/2 cup chopped green bell pepper
- 1/4 cup chopped celery
- 3 tablespoons chopped parsley
- 3 tablespoons chopped pimento
- 1 7-ounce cans sliced mushrooms, drained
- 2 1/2 cups cooked chicken, diced
- 3 cups chicken broth
- 1/2 cup dairy sour cream
- 1/2 cup sliced water chestnuts
- 1/2 cup slivered almonds
- 1/4 teaspoon dried sage
- 1/4 teaspoon dried thyme, crumbled
  Pinch ground black pepper

PREHEAT OVEN TO 350°F

Cook the wild rice according to package directions, and set aside. In a saucepan, melt butter over medium heat. Add onion, garlic and green pepper; stir and cook until soft. Add celery; stir and cook 1 minute. Place all ingredients except rice into a large bowl; mix well. Blend in rice a little at a time. Spoon mixture into a lightly buttered 2 1/2-quart glass baking dish. Cover and bake 50 minutes. Serves 6.

Serve green salad, steamed broccoli and jellied cranberry sauce with this delicious chicken hot dish.

Curried Chicken Hot Dish

4 cups cooked long grain regular rice

2 cups cooked cubed chicken, or cooked turkey

1/2 cup cooked cubed smoked sausage or cooked ham

1 8-ounce can water chestnut, drained and coarsely chopped

1 10 3/4-ounce can condensed cream of chicken soup, undiluted

1 1/2 cups whole milk

1/2 cup mayonnaise (not salad dressing)

1/4 cup minced fresh parsley

2 tablespoons minced yellow onion

3/4 teaspoon salt

1/4 teaspoon curry powder, or to taste

6 tablespoons sliced almonds

PREHEAT OVEN TO 350°F

Spoon rice into a greased 13x9x2-inch baking dish. Top evenly with chicken, sausage and water chestnuts. In a bowl, combine remaining ingredients except almonds; mix well, and pour over chicken mixture. Cover and bake 35 minutes or until hot and bubbly. Remove cover; sprinkle with sliced almonds. Bake 5 minutes. Serves 6.

Serve with a salad of mixed greens and hard rolls.

Harriet's Country Chicken

- 1 whole chicken, cut up or 6 chicken breast halves
- 1 envelope dry onion soup mix
- 1 10¾-ounce can chicken rice soup, undiluted
- 1 cup sliced celery
- 1 10¾-ounce can condensed cream of chicken soup, undiluted
- 1 soup can water
- 1 cup uncooked minute rice

PREHEAT OVEN TO 350°F

Place chicken in a buttered 11x7x2-inch baking dish. In a bowl, combine remaining ingredients; mix well. Pour mixture over chicken. Cover with foil. Bake 1½ hours. Uncover, and bake 25 minutes. Serves 6.

Harriet was the Post Mistress for many years in the small town of Perley, Minnesota. The farm she lived on was only a few miles from town, and, like her hot dish...picture-perfect.

Good!

Italian Chicken & Rice

1½ cups water

1 cup raw long grain white rice

1 14½-ounce can tomatoes, cut up undrained

1 8-ounce jar processed cheese spread

1 medium onion, chopped

1½ teaspoons Italian seasoning, divided

1 2½-pound broiler-fryer chicken skinned and cut up

⅔ cup grated Parmesan cheese

PREHEAT OVEN TO 375°F

In a bowl, combine water, rice, tomatoes, cheese spread, onions and 1 teaspoon Italian seasoning; stir well. Spoon mixture into a greased 13x9x2-inch glass baking dish. Arrange chicken on top. Sprinkle with remaining Italian seasoning. Cover and bake 30 minutes. Uncover, and sprinkle with Parmesan cheese. Bake uncovered, 20 minutes or until chicken test done. Serves 4 to 6.

A green salad will complete this Italian meal.

Suggestion: Add artichokes
add garlic

Jean's Yogurt Chicken

1 cup fine dry bread crumbs
1/4 cup grated Parmesan cheese
1 1/2 tablespoons dried minced onion
1 teaspoon garlic powder
1 teaspoon seasoned salt
1/4 teaspoon dried oregano, crushed
1/4 teaspoon dried thyme, crushed
4 skinless whole chicken breasts, cut in half lengthwise
1 8-ounce carton plain yogurt
1/4 cup butter, melted
2 teaspoons sesame seed
1 7-ounce can sliced mushrooms
6 plum tomatoes, cut into wedges
1 10 3/4-ounce can condensed cream of chicken soup, mixed with 1 cup plain yogurt, 1/2 cup chicken broth, 1 teaspoon lemon juice, 1/2 teaspoon Worcestershire sauce, pinch garlic powder and black pepper

PREHEAT OVEN TO 375°F

In a bowl, combine first seven ingredients. Coat chicken with yogurt; roll in crumb mixture. Place meaty side up into a 15x10x1-inch baking dish. Drizzle top with butter. Sprinkle with sesame seed. Bake uncovered about 55 minutes or until chicken is no longer pink and tests done. Drain mushrooms; spoon around edge of dish. Tuck tomato wedges around mushrooms; bake 6 minutes. Place last ingredient mixture into a saucepan. Cook over low heat until thoroughly heated. Spoon sauce over chicken when serving. Serves 8.

Jean attended art classes in Minneapolis...an artistic touch shows in this hot dish! Serve her tangy chicken dish with buttered pasta and a green salad.

Jeanne's Chicken-Mac

1 7-ounce package elbow macaroni, uncooked

2 cups cubed cooked chicken

1 cup shredded cheddar cheese

1 2-ounce jar diced pimientos, or 2 tablespoons chopped roasted sweet red bell pepper

3 tablespoons minced onion

2 cloves garlic, minced

1/2 teaspoon salt

Pinch black pepper

1/2 teaspoon curry powder

1 10³/4-ounce can condensed cream of chicken soup, undiluted

1 cup whole milk

1 4-ounce can mushroom stems and pieces, undrained

PREHEAT OVEN TO 350°F

Place all ingredients into a 2-quart glass baking dish; mix. Cover and bake about 1 hour or until macaroni test done. Serves 4.

Jeanne is a Home Economist. Many years ago, she told me about using uncooked pasta in certain hot dishes...this is one of them. Serve this easy to prepare hot dish with a crisp green salad.

Kathleen's Chicken Hot Dish

5 tablespoons butter

6 tablespoons all-purpose flour

1 3/4 cup whole milk

1 cup canned chicken broth

2 1/2 cups cubed cooked chicken

1 3/4 cups cooked long grain regular white rice

1/2 teaspoon salt

Pinch ground black pepper

1/3 cup chopped green bell pepper

2 tablespoons minced onion

1 5-ounce can mushroom stem and pieces, drained

1/2 cup slivered almonds

PREHEAT OVEN TO 350°F

In a large saucepan, over medium heat, melt butter. Gradually stir in flour; stir and cook 1 minute. Add milk and chicken broth. Bring to a boil, stirring constantly; stir and cook 1 minute. Add remaining ingredients; mix well. Spoon mixture into a 2 1/2-quart glass baking dish. Bake uncovered about 45 to 50 minutes or until very hot and bubbly. Serves 6.

This is a hot dish prepared in minutes. Serve with buttered peas and soft rolls...buttered of course.

Lottie's Chicken Hot Dish

2 cups cubed cooked chicken

1/2 cup chopped onion

2 stalks celery, diced

1 tablespoon chopped pimiento

1 tablespoon fresh lemon juice

1 teaspoon prepared mustard

1/4 teaspoon salt

1/4 teaspoon black pepper

1/2 cup mayonnaise

3 hard boiled eggs, chopped

1/2 cup slivered almonds

2 cups cooked long grain regular white rice

1 10³/4-ounce can condensed cream of chick soup, undiluted

1½ cups crushed potato chips

PREHEAT OVEN TO 375°F

Place all ingredients, except potato chips, in a large bowl. Mix lightly until combined. Spoon mixture into a 13x9x2-inch glass baking dish. Sprinkle with potato chips. Bake uncovered 35 minutes or until very hot. Serves 6.

Serve with buttered green beans and a fresh fruit salad along with warm rolls.

Manie's Chicken Rice Hot Dish

1 cup uncooked wild rice

3 cups water mixed with
   ½ teaspoon salt

1 tablespoon butter

1 cup chopped onions

1 cup thinly sliced celery

1 cup shredded fresh carrots

1 14-ounce can chicken broth

2 cups half & half (light cream)

¼ cup all-purpose flour

2 tablespoons cooking sherry or
   apple juice

¾ teaspoon salt

¼ teaspoon ground black pepper

3 cups cooked cubed chicken

5 tablespoons dried cranberries

5 tablespoons slice natural almonds,
   toasted

PREHEAT OVEN TO 350°F

In a medium saucepan, bring rice and water to a boil. Reduce heat; cover and simmer 50 minutes; drain in a colander. In a saucepan, melt butter over medium heat. Add onions, celery and carrots; stir and cook 10 minutes. Add broth; bring to a boil. Whisk cream and flour in a bowl until smooth; gradually whisk into boiling broth. Stir in sherry, salt and pepper. Bring to a boil. Reduce heat; simmer 5 minutes. Pour mixture into a large bowl. Add chicken and rice. Mix well. Spoon into a shallow 2½-quart baking dish. Cover and bake 40 minutes, stirring once. Remove from oven. Sprinkle with cranberries and almonds. Let stand 10 minutes before serving. Serves 8.

Wild rice, sweet cranberries, and toasted almonds ...they'll purr over this hot dish!

Mexi-Chicken Hot Dish

- 5 tablespoons corn oil
- 12 soft corn tortillas
- 1 cup chopped onions
- 1 cup chopped green bell pepper
- 2 cloves garlic, minced
- 1 10³/4-ounce can cream of chicken soup, undiluted
- 1 10³/4-ounce can cream of mushroom soup, undiluted
- 1 10-ounce can tomatoes and green chilies
- 1/2 teaspoon chili powder
- 1/4 teaspoon salt
- 3 cups shredded cooked chicken
- 1 cup shredded colby cheese
- 1 cup shredded Monterey Jack cheese

PREHEAT OVEN TO 350°F

In a saucepan, heat corn oil. Place tortillas in hot oil, a few seconds, one at a time, to soften. Drain on paper towel. Cut each into 4 even pieces; set aside. Drain all but 2 tablespoons oil from saucepan. Add onions, bell pepper and garlic to same saucepan; stir and cook 2 minutes. In a bowl, combine all ingredients except tortillas and cheese. In a greased 13x9x2-inch baking dish, make layers starting with half the tortillas, half the chicken mixture and half the cheese. Repeat layers, ending with cheese. Bake 45 minutes or until very hot and bubbly. Serves 6.

Tex-Mex cooking is now cooked and enjoyed by many Minnesotans...my husband, who grew up in northern Minnesota, loves this type of food. Serve a lettuce and tomato salad with this hot dish.

Mr. B's Chicken Parmesan

2 eggs, slightly beaten

3/4 cup Italian seasoned dry bread crumbs

4 boneless, skinless chicken breast halves, lightly seasoned with salt

1 28-ounce jar traditional flavor pasta sauce

1 cup shredded Mozzarella cheese

1/4 cup grated Parmesan cheese

Hot cooked pasta

PREHEAT OVEN TO 400°F

Place eggs in a bowl. Place bread crumbs in another bowl. Dip chicken into egg, then coat with bread crumbs. Place into a lightly greased 13x9x2-inch glass baking dish. Bake uncovered 20 minutes. Pour pasta sauce over chicken. Top with Mozzarella cheese. Sprinkle with Parmesan cheese. Bake 15 minutes or until chicken is no longer pink and tests done. Serve immediately over hot cooked pasta. Serves 4.

Serve with steamed broccoli or a crisp green salad.

Mr. Brown's Chicken & Rice

2 tablespoons corn oil

1 cup chopped onions

1/2 medium size green bell pepper, chopped

2 cloves garlic, coarsely chopped

3/4 cup chopped celery

1/4 cup chopped parsley

6 boneless, skinless chicken breast halves, cut into strips

1 cup raw long grain white rice

1 16-ounce can stewed tomatoes, drained, cut up

1 1/2 cups tomato vegetable juice

1 4-ounce can mushroom stems and pieces, drained

1 cup chicken broth

1/2 teaspoon salt

1/4 teaspoon black pepper

PREHEAT OVEN TO 375°F

In a saucepan, heat corn oil over medium heat. Add onions, green pepper, garlic, celery and parsley. Stir and cook 1 minute; remove and set aside. Season chicken with salt and pepper as desired. Add to same saucepan; stir and cook until lightly browned. Remove and set aside. Add rice to same sauce pan; stir and cook 2 minutes. Combine all ingredients into a large bowl. Spoon into a greased 11 1/2x7 1/2x1 3/4-inch glass baking dish. Cover tightly with foil. Bake 1 hour. Uncover and bake 10 minutes. Serves 6.

Mr. Brown will sometime toss a half dozen cleaned raw shrimp in this hot dish along with the chicken. Serve a mixture of salad greens tossed with an Italian-type dressing with this hot dish.

One Dish Chicken 'n Rice

1 10³/4-ounce can condensed cream of mushroom soup, undiluted

³/4 cup whole milk

¹/2 cup water

¹/2 cup uncooked regular white rice

1 5-ounce jar button mushrooms, drained, optional

¹/4 teaspoon paprika

4 boneless, skinless chicken breast halves, lightly seasoned with salt and ground black pepper

PREHEAT OVEN TO 350°F

In a 2-quart shallow glass baking dish, mix together all ingredients except chicken. Place chicken on top of mixture. Cover and bake about 45 minutes or until chicken and rice test done. Serves 4.

This recipe can easily be changed by adding broccoli cuts, grated onion, etc. I first saw the recipe on a soup can...very easy to prepare.

Reunion Chicken Hot Dish

10 cups diced cooked chicken

10 cups chopped celery

2 whole bunches green onions including tops, sliced

2 4-ounce cans chopped green chilies

1 6-ounce can pitted ripe olives, drained and sliced

2 cups slivered almonds

1/4 teaspoon ground black pepper

5 cups shredded cheddar cheese, divided

2 cups mayonnaise

2 cups dairy sour cream

5 cups crushed potato chips

PREHEAT OVEN TO 350°F

In very large bowl, combine the first seven ingredients. Add 2 cups cheese. In another bowl, combine mayonnaise and sour cream; add to chicken mixture; mix. Spoon mixture into two 13x9x2-inch glass baking dishes. Sprinkle evenly with potato chips. Top with remaining cheese. Bake uncovered, 25 to 30 minutes or until very hot. Serves 24.

Here's a lot of hot dish to serve...perfect for when the family gets together again. Serve with a relish tray, including sliced fresh tomatoes, carrot sticks and other fresh vegetables, along with assorted breads and muffins.

Sam's Chicken Divan

1 16-ounce package frozen broccoli cuts, cooked according to package directions, drain

2 cups cubed cooked skinless chicken breast

1 tablespoon toasted slivered almonds

1 10¾-ounce can condensed cream of chicken soup, undiluted

½ cup mayonnaise or salad dressing

1 teaspoon fresh lemon juice

½ cup shredded cheddar cheese

6 tablespoons dry bread crumbs, mixed with 2 tablespoons melted butter

PREHEAT OVEN TO 350°F

Place broccoli into a greased 12x8-inch glass baking dish. Layer chicken over broccoli. Sprinkle with almonds. In a bowl, mix together soup, mayonnaise and lemon juice; spoon over almonds. Sprinkle with cheese. Top with bread crumb mixture. Bake uncovered about 35 minutes or until very hot. Serves 4.

This is a good company dish. Serve with a nice salad and rolls. Sam will often add cooked rice on bottom, then layer like above.

Scalloped Chicken Hot Dish

12 slices white bread, cubed

1 cup cracker crumbs

3 cups chicken broth

3 eggs, lightly beaten

1 teaspoon salt

1/8 teaspoon ground black pepper

3/4 cup diced celery

1/4 cup chopped onions

3 cups cubed cooked chicken

1 8-ounce can sliced mushrooms, drained

1/2 cup cracker crumbs, mixed with 1 tablespoon melted butter

Paprika

PREHEAT OVEN TO 350°F

In a large bowl, combine bread and 1 cup plain cracker crumbs. Gradually stir in broth, eggs, salt pepper, celery, onions, chicken and mushrooms. Place mixture into a 2-quart baking dish. Sprinkle top with cracker crumb mixture. Bake 1 hour. Sprinkle lightly with paprika. Serves 6.

This dish can be prepared a day ahead of time, except the topping, and refrigerated Add topping just before baking.

Tamale-Chicken Hot Dish

1 cup finely crushed corn chips

1 15-ounce can tamales

1 10-ounce can plain chili

1½ cups chopped cooked chicken

1 8-ounce can whole kernel corn, undrained

1 4-ounce can chopped green chilies, drained

1 cup shredded cheddar cheese

PREHEAT OVEN TO 350°F

Sprinkle corn chips evenly onto bottom of an 8-inch square baking dish. Unwrap tamales, and layer over corn chips. In a large bowl, mix together remaining ingredients except cheese; spoon over tamales. Bake 20 minutes. Sprinkle with cheese, bake 5 minutes. Serves 4 to 6.

Serve this hot dish topped with dairy sour cream.

Tex-Mex Chicken and Rice

- 2 cups minute rice, uncooked
- 4 boneless, skinless chicken breast halves cut into bite-size pieces, lightly seasoned with salt
- 1/2 cup minced onions, cooked in butter 2 minutes
- 2 cloves garlic, minced
- 1 4-ounce can diced green chilies, drained
- 1 16-ounce can diced tomatoes, undrained
- 1 8-ounce can tomato sauce
- 1 cup frozen kernel corn, thawed
- 1/4 teaspoon salt
- 1/4 teaspoon chili powder
- 1/4 teaspoon ground cumin

PREHEAT OVEN TO 350°F

Spread rice evenly into a greased 2½-quart glass baking dish. Top with chicken. Sprinkle with onions and garlic. In a bowl, mix together remaining ingredients; spoon over last layer. Cover and bake 1 hour. Serves 4.

Serve this hot dish with a crisp green salad.

Turkey & Beans Hot Dish

- 1 cup chopped onions
- 3 cloves garlic, chopped
- 1 tablespoon corn oil
- 3/4 pound ground turkey
- 1 16-ounce can tomato sauce
- 1/4 cup brown sugar
- 1/4 cup red wine vinegar
- 2 tablespoons prepared horseradish-type mustard
- 1 teaspoon ground cumin
- 1 teaspoon salt
- 1/4 teaspoon black pepper
- 1 16-ounce can red kidney beans, drained
- 1 16-ounce can garbanzo beans, drained
- 1 16-ounce can cut green beans, drained

PREHEAT OVEN TO 325°F

In a saucepan, stir and cook onions in corn oil until just tender. Add garlic and turkey; stir and cook until meat is browned. Add remaining ingredients; place into a 2½-quart round baking dish. Bake 35 to 45 minutes or until thoroughly heated. Serves 4 to 6.

Serve with a tossed salad, spiced apples rings and warm buttered rolls.

Turkey and Brown Rice

- 1 tablespoon olive oil
- 1 cup chopped onions
- 1 tablespoon chopped garlic
- 1 cup uncooked long grain brown rice
- 1 14-ounce can chicken broth
- 1/4 cup water, mixed with 1/2 teaspoon lemon juice
- 1/4 teaspoon dried sage
- 2 tablespoons butter
- 1 pound button mushrooms, sliced
- 1/4 teaspoon salt
- 1/4 teaspoon black pepper
- 3 cups diced cooked turkey
- 1 10-ounce can condensed cream of mushroom soup, mixed with 1/2 cup milk
- 1/4 cup chopped fresh parsley

PREHEAT OVEN TO 400°F

In a saucepan, heat oil over medium heat. Add onions; stir and cook until soft. Add garlic; stir and cook 1 minute. Stir in rice. Gradually add broth, water and sage. Bring to a boil. Reduce heat to low; cover and simmer 40 minutes. In a saucepan, melt butter over medium heat. Add mushrooms; stir and cook 6 minutes; drain. Stir in salt and pepper. Spoon rice into a lightly buttered 2-quart shallow baking dish. Top evenly with turkey. Spoon mushrooms over turkey. Pour soup over mushrooms. Bake about 30 minutes or until bubbly. Cover with foil last 15 minutes. Top with parsley when serving. Serves 6.

If desired, replace the button mushrooms in this hot dish with shiitake mushrooms, stems removed, sliced, and cooked as above 10 minutes.

Turkey-Ham Tetrazzini

6 tablespoons butter

6 tablespoons all-purpose flour

1 quart whole milk

1/4 teaspoon salt

1/4 teaspoon ground black pepper

2 cups diced cooked turkey

2 cups diced cooked ham

1/2 cup diced celery

1/4 cup slivered almonds

1 tablespoon minced onions

1 clove garlic, minced

1 8-ounce package spaghetti, broken, cooked according to package directions, drained

Grated Parmesan cheese

PREHEAT OVEN TO 350°F

In a saucepan, melt butter over medium heat. Gradually stir in flour; stir and cook 1 minute. Gradually stir in milk to a smooth consistency. Stir in salt and black pepper. In a large bowl, mix together remaining ingredients except Parmesan cheese. Add cooked sauce; stir to blend. Pour mixture into a lightly buttered 13x9x2-inch baking dish. Sprinkle top with cheese as desired. Bake 30 minutes. Let stand 5 minutes before serving. Serves 6 to 8.

Serve this hot dish with a crisp green salad and warm hard rolls.

Turkey Lasagne Hot Dish

1/2 12-ounce package lasagne noodles, cooked according to package directions, drained

1 10³/₄-ounce can condensed cream of chicken soup, undiluted

3/4 cup cream

1/2 teaspoon salt

1/2 teaspoon poultry seasoning

2 3-ounce packages cream cheese

1 cup creamed cottage cheese

1/2 cup chopped green onions

1/4 cup minced fresh parsley

2 cups diced cooked turkey

1 cup soft bread crumbs, mixed with 2 tablespoons butter

PREHEAT OVEN TO 350°F

In a large saucepan, combine soup, cream, salt and poultry seasoning. In a bowl, combine cream cheese and cottage cheese. Beat until smooth; add to saucepan. Stir in onions, parsley and turkey. Place half the cooked noodles into a buttered 11x7x2-inch glass baking dish. Spoon half the cheese, turkey mixture over noodles. Repeat layers. Top with bread crumbs. Bake about 40 minutes or until bubbles in center. Remove from oven. Let stand 10 minutes before serving. Serves 6.

This is another good way to use up leftover turkey.

Turkey Noodle Hot Dish

1 8-ounce package wide egg noodles, cooked according to package directions

1 tablespoon butter

1 tablespoon minced onions

1 clove garlic, minced

3 tablespoons all-purpose flour

2½ cups whole milk

1 tablespoon chicken-flavor bouillon granules

½ cup plain yogurt

2 cups cubed cooked turkey

2 cups frozen broccoli cuts, thawed

¼ teaspoon dried sage

1 cup shredded cheddar cheese

PREHEAT OVEN TO 375°F

In a saucepan, melt butter over medium heat. Add onions and garlic; stir and cook 2 minutes. Gradually stir in flour until blended. Stir in milk until smooth. Stir in bouillon granules. Cook and stir until slightly thickened. In a large bowl, combine all ingredients except cheese. Spoon mixture into a lightly greased 2-quart baking dish. Top with shredded cheese. Cover and bake about 30 minutes or until very hot and bubbly. Serves 4 to 6.

Serve this turkey hot dish with crusty bread and a light fresh fruit salad.

Turkey-Stuffing Hot Dish

1¼ cups water

¼ cup butter

3½ cups seasoned stuffing crumbs

1 3-ounce can French fried onions, divided

1 10¾-ounce can condensed cream of celery soup, undiluted

¾ cup whole milk

1¾ cups cubed cooked turkey

1 10-ounce package frozen peas, drained

PREHEAT OVEN TO 350°F

Heat water in a medium saucepan. Add butter; stir until melted. Remove from heat. Stir in stuffing crumbs and ½ can French fried onions. Spoon mixture into a 1½-quart round glass baking dish; press evenly onto bottom and up sides. In a medium bowl, mix together soup, milk, turkey and peas. Pour mixture into stuffing shell. Bake, covered, 30 minutes or until very hot. Top with remaining onions. Bake uncovered until onions are golden brown, about 5 minutes. Serves 4.

Serve this dish with cole slaw and whole-berry cranberry sauce.

Wild Rice Turkey Hot Dish

1 6-ounce package long grain and wild rice mix, cooked according to package directions

1 10-ounce can condensed cream of chicken soup, undiluted

1 cup water

3 cups cubed cooked turkey

1 cup chopped celery

5 tablespoons chopped onions

1 5-ounce can sliced water chestnuts, drained

1 4-ounce can mushroom stems and pieces, drained

3 tablespoons soy sauce

1/4 teaspoon dried thyme

1 1/2 cups buttered soft bread crumbs

2 tablespoons chopped fresh parsley

PREHEAT OVEN TO 350°F

In a bowl, combine cooked rice and remaining ingredients except bread crumbs and parsley; mix well. Spoon mixture into a lightly buttered 3-quart baking dish. Top with bread crumbs. Bake 1 hour. Remove from oven. Sprinkle with parsley. Serves 8.

A good hot dish to make with leftover turkey. Serve with the leftover cranberry sauce, along with steamed fresh broccoli.

BEEF

3-Bean Beef Hot Dish

1 pound ground beef

1/2 pound bacon, chopped

1 cup chopped onions

1/2 cup catsup

1 teaspoon salt

2 teaspoons vinegar

1/2 cup brown sugar

2 teaspoons prepared mustard

1 15-ounce can butter beans, drained

1 18-ounce can oven baked beans

2 16-ounce cans kidney beans, drained

PREHEAT OVEN TO 350°F

In a saucepan, add beef, bacon and onions; stir and cook until beef is browned; drain fat. Mix together all ingredients. Pour mixture into a 3 1/2-quart baking dish. Cover and bake 40 minutes. Serves 6.

This is a main dish...to make a baked bean side dish, just leave out the ground beef.

Ali's Beef Enchiladas

- 1 pound ground beef, lightly seasoned with salt and ground black pepper
- 1/2 cup chopped onions
- 1 cup picante sauce, divided
- 3/4 teaspoon ground cumin
  Corn oil
- 12 corn tortillas
- 3/4 cup shredded cheddar cheese
- 3/4 cup shredded Monterey Jack cheese

PREHEAT OVEN TO 350°F

In a large saucepan, stir and cook beef and onions until beef is browned; drain fat. Stir in 1/2 cup picante sauce and cumin. In a small saucepan, heat about 1/2-inch deep corn oil until very hot. Quickly fry each tortilla in oil to soften, about 2 seconds on each side; drain on paper towels. Spoon about 1/4 cup meat mixture down center of each tortilla; roll and place seam side down into a 13x9x2-inch baking dish. Spoon remaining picante sauce evenly over enchiladas. Top evenly with cheeses. Bake 15 minutes or until very hot. Serves 6.

If desired, substitute flour tortillas...they need no frying. Serve with a lettuce and avocado salad.

Baked Beef Stew

- 2 tablespoons corn oil
- 2 pounds boneless beef chuck, cut into 2-inch chunks, lightly seasoned with salt and pepper
- 2 medium size onions, chopped
- 3 tablespoons all-purpose flour
- 2 cups beef broth
- 3 cloves garlic, minced
- 1/4 teaspoon dried thyme
- 1/4 teaspoon dried marjoram
- 2 potatoes, peeled, cut into chunks
- 1 8-ounce package fresh mushrooms, cooked in butter 2 minutes, drained
- 1 cup sliced carrots and 1/2 cup sliced celery, cooked in 1 tablespoon butter until tender

PREHEAT OVEN TO 325°F

In a saucepan, heat oil. Add seasoned beef; stir and cook until brown. Place into a deep 3 1/2-quart glass baking dish. Add onion to saucepan; stir and cook until light brown; place into baking dish. In same saucepan, gradually stir in flour until blended. Gradually stir in broth; stir and cook until mixture boils and thickens. Add remaining ingredients except carrots and celery; mix well, and pour into baking dish. Cover and bake 2 1/2 hours. Stir in carrots and celery; cover and bake 20 minutes. Serves 6.

Stew is usually cooked on top of the stove...try this method for a change. Serve stew in bowls along with rolls or over hot white cooked rice along with a tossed salad.

Baked Chili Hot Dish

1 pound ground beef

1 cup chopped onions

1 large green bell pepper, chopped

3 large cloves garlic, minced

1 16-ounce can kidney beans, drained

1 16-ounce can kernel corn, drained

1 16-ounce can diced tomatoes, undrained

1 4-ounce can chopped green chilies

2 teaspoons chili powder

1 teaspoon ground cumin

1/2 teaspoon salt

1 cup all-purpose flour

2 teaspoons baking powder

1/4 teaspoon salt

1 cup yellow cornmeal

1/4 cup whole milk

1/4 cup dairy sour cream

1 large egg, beaten

PREHEAT OVEN TO 400F

In a saucepan, stir and cook beef, onions and bell pepper until meat is no longer pink; drain fat. Add garlic; stir and cook 1 minute. Add all but the last seven ingredients. Bring to a boil. Reduce heat. Cover and simmer 15 minutes, stirring occasionally. Spoon mixture into a 13x9x2-inch baking dish. In a bowl, combine flour, baking powder, salt and cornmeal until blended. In another bowl, combine milk, sour cream and egg until blended; add to dry flour ingredients, stirring only to moisten. Drop by teaspoonfuls on top of hot chili. Bake uncovered 20 minutes or until cornbread topping is light golden brown. Serves 8.

Offer additional sour cream when serving this cornbread topped chili. Serve with a crisp salad.

Beef 'n Barley Hot Dish

1 pound ground beef

1 tablespoon corn oil

1 medium onion, chopped

2 cloves garlic, chopped

1 cup uncooked barley

1/2 cup diced celery

1 20-ounce can whole tomatoes, cut up, undrained

2 1/2 cups water

2 teaspoons salt

Pinch ground black pepper

PREHEAT OVEN TO 350°F

In a saucepan, over medium heat, stir and cook ground beef until browned; remove and place into a 2 1/2-quart baking dish. Drain all but 1 tablespoon drippings. Add corn oil, onion, garlic and barley to saucepan; stir and cook until browned. Add remaining ingredients; mix well and stir into ground beef. Bake 2 hours. Serves 6.

This hot dish is a bit like a beef-barley soup I like to make. Serve this hot dish with buttered carrots along with a broccoli salad.

Beef 'n Beans Hot Dish

3 pounds ground beef

1½ cups chopped onions

½ cup chopped celery

3 cloves garlic, minced

2 teaspoons beef bouillon granules, dissolved in 1 cup boiling water

2 28-ounce cans baked beans (the kind with molasses)

1¼ teaspoons salt

½ teaspoon ground black pepper

½ teaspoon Worcestershire sauce

½ pound sliced bacon, crisply cooked, crumbled

PREHEAT OVEN TO 375°F

In a large saucepan, stir and cook beef, onions, and celery until meat is no longer pink; drain fat. Add garlic; stir and cook 1 minute. Add remaining ingredients except bacon. Mix well. Spoon mixture into a 3-quart baking dish. Cover and bake 1 hour. Remove from oven. Stir in half the bacon and sprinkle with remaining half on top. Serves 12.

Serve this beefy hot dish with a salad and warm crusty bread.

Beef 'n Biscuits Hot Dish

- 1 pound ground beef
- 1/2 cup chopped onion
- 1 10 3/4-ounce can condensed cream of mushroom soup, undiluted
- 1 8-ounce package cream cheese, cut up
- 1 12-ounce can whole kernel corn, drained
- 1/4 cup chopped pimiento
- 1/4 teaspoon salt
- Pinch ground black pepper
- 1 7-ounce can refrigerated buttermilk biscuits

PREHEAT OVEN TO 375°F

In a saucepan, brown ground beef; drain. Add onion; stir and cook until tender. Add soup and cream cheese; stir until cheese is melted. Add corn, pimiento, salt and black pepper; mix lightly. Pour mixture into a 1 1/2-quart baking dish. Separate dough into 10 biscuits; cut each one in half crosswise. Place cut side down around the edge of baking dish. Bake about 25 minutes or until biscuits are browned. Serves 6.

Serve a mixed green salad with this hearty meal.

Beef-Corn Lasagne

- 1 pound ground beef
- 1/2 cup finely chopped onions
- 1 16-ounce can whole kernel corn, drained
- 2 cloves garlic, minced
- 1/2 teaspoon salt
- 1 15-ounce can tomato sauce
- 1 cup picante sauce
- 1 tablespoon chili powder
- 1 1/2 teaspoons ground cumin
- 1 16-ounce carton low-fat cottage cheese
- 2 eggs, slightly beaten
- 1/4 cup grated Parmesan cheese
- 1 teaspoon dried oregano, crushed
- 12 corn tortillas
- 1 cup shredded cheddar cheese

PREHEAT OVEN TO 375°F

In a saucepan, stir and cook beef and onions until browned; drain fat. Add corn, garlic, salt, tomato sauce, picante sauce, chili powder and cumin. Simmer 5 minutes, stirring often. In a bowl, mix together cottage cheese, eggs, Parmesan cheese and oregano. Place 6 tortillas on bottom and up sides of a greased 13x9x2-inch glass baking dish, overlapping as necessary. Top with half the beef mixture. Spoon all the cottage cheese over meat layer. Place remaining tortillas over cottage cheese, overlapping as necessary. Top with remaining beef mixture. Bake 35 minutes or until bubbly. Remove from oven. Sprinkle with cheddar cheese. Let stand 10 minutes before serving. Serves 8.

Serve this Tex-Mex lasagne with a green salad.

Beef-Rigatoni Hot Dish

1 tablespoon olive oil

1/2 pound ground beef, lightly seasoned with salt

1 small onion, chopped

2 1/2 cups rigatoni pasta, cooked according to package directions, drained

1 20-ounce jar thick-chunky salsa

1 15-ounce can black beans, drained

1 cup frozen whole kernel corn

1/2 cup shredded Monterey Jack cheese mixed with 1/2 cup shredded cheddar cheese

2 plum tomatoes, thinly sliced

Chopped fresh flat parsley

PREHEAT OVEN TO 350°F

In a large saucepan, heat oil over medium-high heat. Add beef and onions; stir and cook until brown. Drain fat. Add cooked pasta, salsa, black beans and corn to saucepan mixture; mix well. Spoon half the mixture into a greased 4-quart baking dish. Sprinkle with half the cheese. Top with remaining beef mixture. Top with tomatoes. Sprinkle with remaining cheese. Cover and bake 40 minutes. Garnish with chopped parsley as desired. Serves 4 to 6.

Serve this hot dish with salad and garlic bread.

Beef Stroganoff

3 tablespoons butter

2 pounds sirloin steak, cut into thin 1-inch slanting strips, lightly seasoned with salt and ground black pepper

1 large onion, thinly sliced

1 pound fresh mushrooms, sliced

3 tablespoons all-purpose flour

1 1/2 cups beef broth

1/2 cup dry red wine, or apple juice

2 teaspoons paprika

1/4 teaspoon dried dill weed

Pinch ground nutmeg

3 cloves garlic, minced

1 cup dairy sour cream

Cooked buttered noodles

Minced parsley

PREHEAT OVEN TO 350°F

Melt butter in a large saucepan. Add beef; stir and cook until browned; place into a 3-quart glass baking dish. In same saucepan, stir and cook onion and mushrooms until tender. Stir in flour until blended. Stir in remaining ingredients except sour cream, noodles and parsley. Quickly bring to a boil. Remove from heat; pour over beef. Cover and bake 1 1/2 hours or until meat is very tender. Remove from oven. Gradually stir in sour cream. Serve over cooked noodles, and garnish with parsley as desired. Serves 6.

A classic...you can use other cuts of beef for stroganoff if desired.

Biscuit Topped Beef Hot Dish

- 1 pound ground beef
- 1 medium size onion, chopped
- 2 cloves garlic, chopped
- 3/4 cup water
- 1/2 teaspoon salt or to taste
- 1/4 teaspoon black pepper
- 1 8-ounce can tomato sauce
- 1 8-ounce can tomato paste
- 1 9-ounce package frozen mixed vegetables, thawed
- 2 cups shredded Mozzarella cheese, divided
- 1 10-ounce can refrigerated buttermilk biscuits
- 1 tablespoon butter, melted
- 1/2 teaspoon dried oregano leaves, crushed

PREHEAT OVEN TO 375°F

In a large saucepan, stir and cook ground beef and onion until browned; drain. Add garlic; stir and cook 1 minute. Stir in water, salt, pepper, tomato sauce and tomato paste; bring to a boil, then lower heat and simmer 15 minutes, stirring often. Stir in vegetables and 1 1/2 cups cheese. Spoon mixture into a greased 2-quart glass baking dish. Separate dough into 10 biscuits. Separate each biscuit into 2 layers. Place biscuits near outer edge of meat mixture, overlapping slightly. Sprinkle remaining cheese in center and around edge. Gently brush biscuits with melted butter and sprinkle with oregano. Bake about 25 minutes or until biscuits are golden brown. Serves 6.

A crisp green salad will complete this tasty, easy to prepare, Italian-flavored meal.

Cajun John's Jambalaya

1 1/4 cups regular long grain white rice, uncooked

2 tablespoons corn oil

1 cup chopped onions

1 large green bell pepper, chopped

3 cloves garlic, chopped

2 stalks celery, chopped

3/4 pound smoked sausage, sliced into 1/2-inch pieces

1 pound raw, medium size peeled fresh shrimp, cut in half crosswise

2 14-ounce cans stewed tomatoes, chopped, undrained

1/2 teaspoon salt

1/4 teaspoon cayenne pepper, scant

1 1/2 cups water or chicken stock

PREHEAT OVEN TO 350°F

Spread rice evenly on bottom of a 3 1/2-quart glass baking dish. In a large saucepan, heat corn oil over high heat. Add onion and bell pepper; stir and cook 1 minute. Add garlic; stir and cook a few seconds. Remove vegetables from saucepan; place into a large bowl. Add sausage to saucepan; stir and cook 3 minutes; drain all but 1 tablespoon drippings. Add all ingredients, except water, to the large bowl mixture; stir to mix. Spoon mixture evenly over rice. Pour water over top. Cover tightly; bake about 1 hour or until rice is tender. Serves 6.

Jambalaya means a mixture. You can add cooked cubed chicken and pork to this dish if desired. Serve with a crisp tossed salad and fresh French bread to complete this cajun meal.

Cheesy Spaghetti Hot Dish

1 tablespoon butter

1 cup chopped onions

1 cup chopped green bell pepper

1 pound ground beef

1 28-ounce and tomatoes, including liquid, chopped

1 4-ounce can mushroom stems and pieces, drained

1 3-ounce can sliced ripe olives, drained

1 1/2 teaspoons dried oregano

1 12-ounce package spaghetti, cooked according to package directions, drained

2 cups shredded cheddar cheese

1 10-ounce can cream of mushroom soup, mixed with 1/4 cup water

1/4 cup grated Parmesan cheese

PREHEAT OVEN TO 350°F

In a large saucepan, melt butter over medium heat. Add onions and green bell pepper; stir and cook until soft. Add ground beef; stir and cook until browned; drain all but 1 tablespoon drippings. Add tomatoes, mushrooms, olives, and oregano. Simmer uncovered 10 minutes. Place half the cooked spaghetti into a greased 13x9x2-inch baking dish. Top with half the vegetable-meat mixture. Sprinkle with 1 cup cheddar cheese. Repeat layers. Pour soup mixture over all. Sprinkle with Parmesan cheese. Bake uncovered 30 to 35 minutes or until hot and bubbly. Serves 8.

A crisp green salad and warm garlic bread will go well with this spaghetti hot dish.

Chow Mein Hot Dish

1 pound ground beef

1/2 cup chopped celery

1/4 cup chopped onions

3/4 cup uncooked minute rice

1 1/4 cups boiling water

1/2 teaspoon salt

1 10 3/4-ounce can condensed chicken and rice soup, undiluted

1 4-ounce sliced mushrooms, drained

1 tablespoon brown sugar

2 tablespoons soy sauce

1 teaspoon margarine

1 1/2 cups chow mein noodles

PREHEAT OVEN TO 350°F

In a saucepan, over medium heat, stir and cook ground beef, celery and onions until meat is browned; drain. Place rice into a lightly greased 2-quart baking dish. Pour boiling water over rice. Stir in remaining ingredients except chow mein noodles. Cover and bake 30 minutes. Remove cover. Stir; bake uncovered 30 minutes. Stir in chow mein noodles just before serving. Serves 4.

A tasty hot dish so easy to prepare. Thanks Evie.

Classic Italian Lasagne

- ½ pound ground beef
- ½ pound ground lean pork
- ¾ cup chopped onions
- 3 cloves garlic, crushed
- 1 28-ounce can whole tomatoes, undrained
- 2 6-ounce cans tomato paste
- ½ teaspoon salt
- 1 teaspoon dried basil leaves
- ½ teaspoon dried oregano leaves
- ¼ teaspoon crushed dried red pepper
- 16 pieces uncooked lasagne
- 1¾ cup Ricotta or creamed cottage cheese
- 2 cups shredded Mozzarella cheese, divided
- ¼ cup grated Parmesan cheese
- ¼ cup chopped fresh parsley
- 2 eggs
- ¼ teaspoon ground black pepper

PREHEAT OVEN TO 350°F

In a large saucepan, stir and cook meat, onions and garlic until meat is browned; drain. Add tomatoes, tomato paste, salt, basil, oregano and red pepper; simmer sauce, covered, 20 minutes; set aside. Cook lasagne according to package directions; drain. Lay flat on foil to cool. In a bowl, stir together Ricotta cheese, 1 cup Mozzarella cheese, Parmesan cheese, parsley, eggs and ground black pepper. Spread 1 cup sauce on bottom of a 13x9x2-inch baking dish. Arrange 4 pasta pieces lengthwise over sauce, overlapping edges. Spread ⅓ cheese mixture and 1 cup sauce over pasta. Repeat layers twice, beginning with pasta. Top with layer of pasta, remaining sauce and remaining 1 cup Mozzarella cheese. Cover with foil. Bake 30 minutes or until hot and bubbly. Remove foil; bake 10 minutes. Let stand 10 minutes before cutting. Serves 12.

Salad and French bread will complete this meal.

Corned Beef Hot Dish

2 cups elbow macaroni

1 tablespoon butter

1 12-ounce can corned beef, chopped

1/4 pound cheddar cheese, shredded

1/2 cup chopped onion

1 10³/4-ounce can condensed cream of chicken soup, undiluted

1 cup whole milk

1/2 cup finely chopped celery

Potato chips

PREHEAT OVEN TO 350°F

Cook macaroni 3 minutes less than package directions; drain. Place into a large bowl; add butter; stir. Add remaining ingredients except potato chips; mix well. Spoon mixture into a greased 2¹/2-quart baking dish. Crumble enough potato chips to cover top. Bake uncovered about 1 hour or until very hot and bubbly. Serves 4.

This hot dish comes from the Kirkebo Lutheran Church cookbook, Perley, Minnesota, the 100th anniversary edition.

Cotton Lake Hot Dish

1   7-ounce package macaroni, cooked 3 minutes less than package directions, drained

1   tablespoon corn oil

1   medium onion, chopped

1/2 medium green bell pepper, chopped

1   pound ground beef

1/4 teaspoon salt

   Pinch ground black pepper

2   8-ounce cans tomato sauce

1/4 pound American cheese, cut up

PREHEAT OVEN TO 350°F

In a saucepan, add corn oil, onions and green pepper; stir and cook until soft. Add ground beef; stir and cook until no longer pink. Drain all but 1 tablespoon drippings. Add salt, pepper, tomato sauce and cheese; stir and cook 2 minutes. Combine all ingredients in a 2 1/2-quart glass baking dish. Bake uncovered 30 to 35 minutes or until hot and bubbly. Serves 4.

We spent many summers at our cottage on Cotton Lake, located near Detroit Lakes, Minnesota. When we didn't have any real luck fishing, we turned to this hot dish...along with a healing dessert!

Dried Beef Hot Dish

2 cups large size elbow macaroni, cooked according to package directions, less 3 minutes cooking time, set aside

2 10³/4 cans condensed cream of mushroom soup, undiluted

³/4 cup whole milk

1 cup salad dressing (mayonnaise)

1 cup grated cheddar cheese

3 hard boiled eggs, chopped

2 2-ounce packages dried beef, cut up

PREHEAT OVEN TO 350°F

In a large bowl, mix together soup, milk and salad dressing until well blended. Add cheese, eggs, beef and macaroni; mix well. Pour mixture into a greased 2-quart glass baking dish. Bake uncovered about 35 minutes or until thoroughly heated. Serves 6.

I have not found many hot dishes using dried beef. My good friend Karan, who lives in Columbia Heights, Minnesota, as a young bride, served a dried beef dish to her husband, many times...creamed beef on toast. This dried beef hot dish is easy to pre-pare...and very tasty.

Eggplant Moussaka

1 cup chopped onions

8 tablespoons olive oil, divided

2 cloves garlic, chopped

1/2 pound ground beef

1/4 pound ground lamb

1/4 pound each ground pork

1/4 teaspoon salt or to taste

1 egg, slightly beaten

2 1-pound eggplants, peeled, cut into 1/4-inch slices, lightly salted

All-purpose flour

3 eggs, well beaten

2 tablespoons butter

1/4 cup all-purpose flour, mixed with pinch salt, pinch ground nutmeg

1 1/2 cups whole milk

2 egg yolks

1/4 cup grated Parmesan cheese

PREHEAT OVEN TO 375°F

In a saucepan, stir and cook onions in 2 tablespoons olive oil until tender. Add garlic, meat, salt, and 1 slightly beaten egg; stir and cook until browned; drain fat. Dredge eggplant slices into plain flour; dip into well beaten eggs, a few at a time; fry in remaining olive oil, to brown both sides. Place a layer of fried eggplant on bottom of a 13x9x2-inch glass baking dish, then a layer of meat mixture; repeat layers ending with eggplant. In a small saucepan, melt butter. Stir in flour mixture until blended. Add milk, stirring constantly until thickened. Remove from heat; beat in egg yolks. Stir in cheese; pour over eggplant. Bake uncovered 1 hour. Serves 6.

Serve this Greek hot dish topped with dairy sour cream as desired.

Good Beef 'n Rice Hot Dish

1 pound ground beef
1 large onion, chopped
1/2 cup uncooked regular white rice
1 teaspoon salt
    Pinch ground black pepper
1 1/2 cups tomato juice

In a large saucepan, stir and cook ground beef and onion until browned; drain most, but not all, of the fat. Add remaining ingredients; mix well. Spoon mixture into a 2 1/2-quart baking dish. Cover and bake 1 hour. Serves 6.

This is a hot dish we would put in the oven when we were in a hurry to go fishing. We served it with green salad, canned corn and bread...buttered of course.

Hannah's Hot Dish

1½ pounds ground beef, seasoned with a scant pinch of salt and black pepper

½ cup chopped onions 2 cups chopped celery, blanched

1 10¾-ounce can cream of mushroom soup, undiluted

1 10¾-ounce can cream of chicken soup, undiluted

1 14-ounce can bean sprouts, drained

1 cup uncooked long grain regular white rice

2 cups water

¼ cup soy sauce

Pinch ground black pepper

PREHEAT OVEN TO 350°F

In a saucepan, over medium heat, stir and cook ground beef and onions until browned. Drain all but 2 tablespoons of drippings. In a large bowl, combine all ingredients; mix well. Pour mixture into a 3-quart glass baking dish or a covered roasting pan. Cover tightly with foil. Bake 2 hours. Serves 8.

Hannah is my husband's mother. She made this hot dish when the family gathered from all corners of the country...she never titled it, just called it a good hot dish. We all agree.

Hungarian Goulash

- 2 tablespoons corn oil
- 1 cup chopped onions
- 2½ pounds beef shoulder, cut into 1½-inch cubes
- 2 cloves garlic, chopped
- ½ cup chopped green bell pepper
- 2 tablespoons all-purpose flour
- ½ cup water
- 1 14½-ounce can diced tomatoes
- 2 teaspoons paprika
- ½ teaspoon coarsely ground black pepper
- ¼ teaspoon dried thyme
- Pinch cayenne pepper
- Salt to taste
- 1 cup dairy sour cream
- Cooked noodles or spätzle

PREHEAT OVEN TO 325°F

Heat corn oil in a saucepan. Add onions; stir and cook, over medium heat, until browned; remove from pan. Add beef to same saucepan; stir and cook until browned on all sides. Add garlic and bell pepper; stir and cook 1 minute. Stir in flour until well blended. Stir in water. Add cooked onions and remaining ingredients, except sour cream; mix well. Pour mixture into a 2½-quart glass baking dish. Cover and bake 1½ hours. Remove from oven; stir in sour cream. Cover and bake 30 minutes. Serve over hot cooked noodles or cooked spätzle. Serves 6.

This dish has been around for ages. Paprika give this Hungarian stew its special flavor. Serve with choice of bread and butter.

Jeanne's Beef Hot Dish

- 1 pound ground beef lightly seasoned with salt and ground black pepper
- 1 small onion, chopped
- 1 heaping cup uncooked small thin egg noodles
- 1 10³/4-ounce can tomato soup, undiluted
- 1 10³/4-ounce can condensed chicken noodle soup, undiluted
- 2 slices American cheese, cut up

PREHEAT OVEN TO 375°F

In a saucepan, stir and cook ground beef and onion until browned; drain most of the fat. In a bowl, combine all ingredients except cheese; mix well. Spoon mixture into a greased 2½-quart baking dish. Bake 1 hour. Top with cheese a few minutes before removing from oven. Serves 4.

Jeanne grew up on a farm near Lindstrom, Minnesota....she taught Home Ec in Minneapolis. Known for more elaborate hot dishes...she calls this one her "extra easy" hot dish.

Millie's Wild Rice Hot Dish

2 slices bread, toasted
Whole milk
1 egg, slightly beaten
1/2 pound ground beef
1/2 pound ground lean pork
1 medium onion, grated
Salt and ground black pepper
2 tablespoons butter
1 cup wild rice, washed
Water
1 cup chopped celery
1/2 medium green bell pepper, diced
Salt to taste
1 cup sliced mushrooms
1 10³/4-ounce can condensed cream of mushroom soup, undiluted
1/2 soup can water
1/4 cup grated Parmesan cheese

PREHEAT OVEN TO 350°F

In a bowl, crumb bread into enough milk to soak well. Add egg, meat, grated onion, salt and pepper to taste. Form into meatballs. Melt butter in a saucepan. Add meatballs; brown lightly. In a deep saucepan, add rice and enough water to cover. Add celery, green bell pepper and salt to taste. Bring to a boil; reduce heat, and simmer until rice is almost tender. Add sliced mushrooms, mushroom soup, water and cheese; stir to mix. Place mixture into a 2¹/2-quart baking dish. Arrange meatballs over ice, pressing gently into rice mixture. Cover and bake about 45 minutes or until rice is tender and meat no longer pink. Serves 6.

Cousin Mildred Distad taught music most of her life. She retired in Moorhead, Minnesota. She loved trying new hot dishes...this is one of them.

New Shepherd's Pie

- 1 tablespoon corn oil
- 1 medium size onion, chopped
- 1 pound lean ground beef
- 2 cloves garlic, chopped
- 1 12-ounce jar homestyle beef gravy, or homemade beef gravy
- 2 tablespoons ketchup
- 1 9-ounce package frozen mixed vegetables
- 2 cups water
- 2 tablespoons butter
- 1/4 teaspoon salt
- 2 1/2 cups instant mashed potato flakes, or equal amount homemade
- 1 cup whole milk
- 1 egg, slightly beaten
- 1/2 cup shredded cheddar cheese
- Paprika

PREHEAT OVEN TO 375°F

In a saucepan, heat oil. Add onions and beef; stir and cook until beef is thoroughly cooked. Drain fat. Add garlic, gravy, ketchup and vegetables. Bring to a boil; reduce heat; simmer 8 minutes. Place mixture into a 2-quart glass baking dish. In a saucepan, bring water to a boil. Add butter and salt; stir. Remove from heat. Stir in potato flakes and milk. Let rest 5 minutes. Add egg to potatoes; mix well. Add cheese; mix well. Spoon potatoes evenly over top of meat mixture. Sprinkle lightly with paprika. Bake about 25 minutes or until potatoes are set and lightly browned. Serves 4.

The original shepherd's pie was made with a thin lining of mashed potatoes on bottom of dish, filled with cooked cubed lamb and lamb gravy, topped with more mashed potatoes.

Quick Taco Hot Dish

- 1 pound lean ground beef, seasoned with 1/4 teaspoon salt
- 1 small onion, minced
- 1 10³/4-ounce can condensed tomato soup, undiluted
- 1 cup thick and chunky salsa
- 1/2 cup whole milk
- 8 6-inch corn tortillas, cut into 1-inch pieces
- 1 cup shredded cheddar cheese, divided

  Fresh diced tomatoes

  Shredded lettuce

PREHEAT OVEN TO 400°F

In a saucepan, over medium heat, stir and cook ground beef and onions until browned; drain fat. Add soup, salsa, milk, tortillas and half the cheese. Spoon into a shallow 2-quart glass baking dish. Cover and bake 30 minutes or until very hot. Remove from oven. Sprinkle with remaining cheese. When serving, top with tomatoes and lettuce as desired. Serves 4.

For an extra taste treat, top with dairy sour cream.

Ravioli Hot Dish

- 1 pound ground beef, lightly seasoned with salt
- 2 tablespoons finely chopped onion
- 1 28-ounce jar spaghetti sauce
- 1 25-ounce package frozen cheese ravioli
- 1½ cups shredded Mozzarella cheese

PREHEAT OVEN TO 425°F

In a saucepan, over medium heat, stir and cook beef and onions until browned; drain fat. In an 11x7x2-inch glass baking dish, layer 1 cup spaghetti sauce, half of the frozen ravioli, half of beef mixture and half of cheese. Then layer with 1 cup spaghetti sauce, remaining ravioli, and remaining beef mixture. Pour remaining spaghetti sauce on top. Bake uncovered 30 to 35 minutes. Top with remaining cheese; bake until cheese is melted. Serves 4.

A salad and garlic bread will go nicely with this ravioli hot dish...almost lasagne!

Reuben Hot Dish

1 8-ounce package wide noodles, cooked according to package directions, drained, then mixed with 3 tablespoons soft butter

1 pound sauerkraut, drained

2 cups chopped corned beef

2 medium tomatoes, peeled, sliced

1/4 cup thousand island salad dressing

2 cups shredded Swiss cheese

4 crisp rye crackers, crushed

1/4 teaspoon caraway seeds, more if desired

PREHEAT OVEN TO 350°F

In a greased 13x9x2-inch glass baking dish, layer noodles, sauerkraut, corned beef and tomatoes. Dot with salad dressing and sprinkle with cheese. Top with cracker crumbs and caraway seeds. Bake covered 40 minutes. Uncover; bake 15 minutes or until hot and bubbly. Serves 6 to 8.

If you know someone who loves Reuben sandwiches ...be sure to try this hot dish.

Ruth's Beef 'n Cabbage

- 1½ pounds ground beef, seasoned with ¼ teaspoon salt
- 1 cup chopped onions
- 2 cloves garlic, chopped
- ½ medium size green bell pepper, chopped
- ½ cup chopped celery
- ½ cup uncooked long grain regular white rice
- 1 teaspoon salt
- ¼ teaspoon ground black pepper
- 1 medium size cabbage, sliced
- 1 12-ounce can tomato-vegetable juice

PREHEAT OVEN TO 350°F

In a saucepan, over medium heat, stir and cook beef, onions, garlic, bell pepper and celery until meat is browned; drain half the fat. Add rice, salt and black pepper; mix well. In a 2½-quart glass baking dish, layer sliced cabbage and meat mixture, ending with cabbage. Pour tomato-vegetable juice over all. Cover and bake 1½ hours. Serves 6.

Use the food processor to slice the cabbage. Serve this hot dish with fresh sliced tomatoes, fresh buttered corn and warm rolls.

Sam's Tamale Pie

- 1 pound ground beef, lightly seasoned with salt
- 1/2 pound bulk pork sausage
- 1 tablespoon corn oil
- 1 cup chopped onions
- 2 cloves garlic, finely chopped
- 1 28-ounce can tomatoes, cut up
- 1 10-ounce package frozen corn
- 1 1/2 cup shredded cheddar cheese, divided
- 1 tablespoon chili powder
- 3/4 teaspoon ground cumin
- 1/2 cup sliced black olives
- 2 tablespoons canned diced green chilies
- 1 cup whole milk
- 2 eggs, slightly beaten
- 1 cup cornmeal, plus pinch salt

PREHEAT OVEN TO 375°F

In a saucepan, stir and cook beef and sausage until browned; drain fat. Add corn oil to saucepan. Add onions and garlic; stir and cook, over medium-high heat 2 minutes. Add tomatoes, corn, 1/2 cup cheddar cheese, chili powder and cumin; stir well. Simmer 10 minutes; stir in olives and green chilies. Pour into a 13x9x2-inch glass baking dish. In a bowl, mix together milk, eggs and cornmeal. Spoon mixture evenly over meat. Sprinkle with 1 cup cheddar cheese. Bake uncovered 40 to 50 minutes or until top is light brown. Serves 6.

This cornbread-topped hot dish is meaty, a little spicy but not too hot. Like Sam...unforgettable.

Simple Pasta Hot Dish

- 1 pound ground beef
- 5 cups cooked pasta such as macaroni or spirals
- 1 30-ounce jar spaghetti sauce
- 1/2 cup grated Parmesan cheese
- 1 8-ounce package shredded Mozzarella cheese

PREHEAT OVEN TO 375°F

In a large saucepan, stir and cook beef until done; drain fat. Stir in pasta, spaghetti sauce and grated cheese. Spoon mixture into a 13x9x2-inch baking dish. Top with shredded cheese. Bake uncovered 20 minutes. Serves 4.

This is so easy to prepare...serve with crisp salad.

Spanish Rice Hot Dish

1 pound ground beef, seasoned with 1/4 teaspoon salt, and pinch ground black pepper

2 tablespoons olive oil or margarine

1 medium size onion, chopped

1/2 cup chopped green bell pepper

1 cup diced celery

2 8-ounce cans tomato sauce

1 teaspoon salt

1 cup long grain white rice, cooked according to package directions

PREHEAT OVEN TO 375°F

In a saucepan, over medium heat, stir and cook ground beef until well browned; drain fat. Place beef into a 2-quart baking dish. Heat olive oil in same saucepan. Add onions, green pepper and celery; stir and cook 5 minutes. Add tomato sauce and salt. Cover; simmer 10 minutes, stirring occasionally. Spoon into baking dish. Add cooked rice; stir until well mixed. Bake uncovered 25 minutes. Serves 4.

Spanish rice, an old favorite hot dish. Serve with a tossed green salad.

Spanish Rice with Mushrooms

¼ cup olive oil, divided

1 8-ounce package beef-flavor rice mix, uncooked

1 pound ground beef

½ cup chopped onion

¼ cup diced green bell pepper

¼ cup sliced stuffed olives

2 16-ounce cans stewed tomatoes

1 6-ounce can sliced mushrooms, drained

1 cup water

Salt and black pepper to taste

PREHEAT OVEN TO 350°F

In a saucepan, over medium heat, add 3 tablespoons olive oil. Add rice. (Do not add the seasoning mix pack yet.) Stir and cook until golden. Pour mixture into a 2-quart baking dish. Sprinkle seasoning mix from pack over rice. Heat remaining olive oil to same saucepan. Add beef, onion and green pepper; stir and cook until brown. Drain; add to baking dish. Add olives, tomatoes, mushrooms and water. Mix well. Cover and bake 45 minutes or until rice is tender. Uncover and fluff mixture with a fork. Season with salt and pepper as desired. Serves 6.

This hot dish is versatile...omit the olives and increase the green pepper, if desired. Serve with a green salad and bread of choice.

String Hot Dish

1 pound ground beef

1 medium size onion, chopped

1/4 cup chopped green bell pepper

1 16-ounce jar spaghetti sauce

8 ounces spaghetti, cooked according to package directions, drained

6 tablespoons Parmesan cheese

2 eggs, beaten

2 teaspoons butter

1 cup cottage cheese

1/2 cup shredded Mozzarella cheese

PREHEAT OVEN TO 350°F

In a saucepan, over medium-high heat, stir and cook beef, onion and green bell pepper until meat is browned; drain fat. Stir in spaghetti sauce; mix well. In a large bowl, mix together hot spaghetti, Parmesan cheese, eggs and butter. Spoon mixture onto bottom of a 13x9x2-inch glass baking dish. Spread cottage over top. Pour meat sauce mixture over cottage cheese. Sprinkle top evenly with Mozzarella cheese. Bake uncovered about 20 minutes or until cheese melts. Serves 6.

Salad and warm garlic bread will go well with this string (spaghetti) hot dish.

Swedish Meatballs

¹/₂ cup minced onions

2 tablespoons butter

1¹/₄ pounds ground beef

¹/₄ pound ground pork

¹/₄ teaspoon salt or to taste

¹/₄ teaspoon ground black pepper

Pinch ground nutmeg

1 cup unseasoned bread crumbs

¹/₂ cup whole milk

1 egg, plus 1 yolk, slightly beaten

2 tablespoons margarine or butter

2 tablespoons all-purpose flour, mixed with ¹/₄ teaspoon salt, ¹/₄ teaspoon paprika and pinch of ground black pepper

1¹/₄ cups skim milk

Hot cooked noodles, buttered

PREHEAT OVEN TO 350°F

In a medium saucepan, stir and cook onions in butter until soft, but not brown; spoon mixture into a large bowl. Add next 8 ingredients to bowl. Mix gently, and form into 1-inch meatballs; place in same saucepan; brown on all sides. Place browned meatballs into a greased 2¹/₂-quart glass baking dish. In a small saucepan melt margarine over medium heat. Gradually add flour mixture, stirring constantly until blended. Gradually stir in milk; stir and cook until thickened. Pour over meatballs. Cover and bake 50 minutes. Serve over hot cooked buttered noodles. Serves 6.

Swedish meatballs are very popular in Minnesota...there are many blonde Swedes living here! Serve this hot dish with buttered peas and favorite bread.

Taco Hot Dish

2 pounds ground beef

1 cup chopped onions

3 cloves garlic, chopped

1 15-ounce can tomato sauce

1 1¼-ounce taco seasoning mix

1 16-ounce can kidney beans, undrained

1 12-ounce package corn chips

2 cups shredded cheddar cheese

PREHEAT OVEN TO 350°F

In a saucepan, over medium heat, add ground beef, onions and garlic; stir and cook until meat is slightly browned; drain most of the drippings, but not all. Add tomato sauce and taco seasoning mix; simmer 25 minutes, stirring often. Stir in beans. In a shallow 2½-quart baking dish, make layers starting with half the meat mixture, half the corn chips, and half the cheese. Repeat layers, ending with cheese. Bake 45 minutes. Serves 8.

Tacos were hard to find in Minnesota in the early '50s...now a favorite food. Serve this taco-like hot dish with shredded lettuce, diced onions, chopped tomatoes, olives and sour cream.

Taco Style Lasagne

1 pound ground beef, turkey or chicken

1 tablespoon instant minced onion

1 15-ounce can tomato sauce with tomato bits

1 16-ounce jar thick & chunky salsa

12 pieces oven ready lasagne, uncooked

4 cups shredded sharp cheddar cheese, divided

1/4 cup tortilla chips, optional

1/4 cup sliced ripe black olives

PREHEAT OVEN TO 375°F

In a large saucepan, stir and cook meat and onion until meat is done; drain fat. In a bowl, stir together tomato sauce and salsa; spread 1/2 cup on bottom of a 13x9x2-inch baking dish. Add remaining tomato sauce mixture to meat; heat to boiling. Place 3 pieces uncooked pasta crosswise in dish. Pieces should not overlap or touch side of pan...pasta will expand when baked. Spread about 2/3 cup meat sauce over pasta, covering pasta completely. Sprinkle evenly with 1 cup cheese. Repeat layers twice, beginning and ending with pasta. Top with remaining 3 pasta pieces. Spread remaining sauce on top, covering pasta completely; sprinkle with remaining cheese. Cover with foil. Bake 35 minutes or until hot and bubbly. Let stand 10 minutes before cutting. Sprinkle with tortilla chips and olives, if desired. Serves 8 to 10.

Serve with a crisp green salad and favorite bread.

Tater Tot Hot Dish

1 pound ground beef, lightly seasoned with black pepper

¹/₂ cup chopped onions, optional

1 10³/₄-ounce can condensed cream of chicken soup, undiluted

1 cup canned green beans, peas, or creamed corn,

1 10³/₄-ounce can condensed cream of mushroom soup, undiluted

Frozen tater tots

PREHEAT OVEN TO 350°F

Spread raw ground beef onto bottom of a greased 9x9-inch baking dish. Sprinkle evenly with onions. Top with cream of chicken soup, then green beans. Spread with enough frozen tater tots to cover top. Pour cream of mushroom soup over all. Bake 55 minutes. Serves 4.

This hot dish was a hit when frozen tater tots came out years ago...still going. Serve with crusty rolls.

Wild Rice-Beef Hot Dish

- 3 cups water
- 1 cup uncooked wild rice, rinsed
- 1 teaspoon salt
- 2 tablespoons butter, divided
- 1 pound ground beef
- 3 cups sliced fresh mushrooms
- 2 stalks celery, chopped
- 1/2 cup chopped onions
- 1 10 3/4-ounce can cream of mushroom soup, undiluted
- 1 1/4 cups water
- 1/8 teaspoon black pepper
- 3 tablespoons soy sauce

PREHEAT OVEN TO 375°F

In a saucepan, bring water to boiling. Add rice and salt; simmer 40 minutes, do not drain. Set aside. In a sauce pan, over medium heat, melt 1 tablespoon butter. Add ground beef; stir and cook until browned; drain and set aside. In the same saucepan, melt remaining butter. Add mushrooms; stir and cook 3 minutes. In a bowl, combine all ingredients; mix well. Spoon mixture into a 13x9x2-inch glass baking dish. Bake 55 minutes. Serves 6.

Minnesota is famous for genuine wild rice...serve this hot dish with a crisp green salad and warm crusty bread...buttered of course.

Wild Rice with Pine Nuts

1½ pounds ground beef
1 pound bulk pork sausage
3 tablespoons butter
1 green bell pepper, chopped
1¼ cups finely chopped onions
3 cups chopped celery
8 cups chicken broth
¾ cups wild rice
¾ cup long grain regular white rice
1 cup pine nuts
Salt and black pepper to taste

PREHEAT OVEN TO 350°F

In a large saucepan, stir and cook beef and sausage until browned; drain fat. In another saucepan, add butter, green bell pepper, onions and celery; stir and cook until just tender. In a large saucepan, mix together broth, rice, meat, vegetables, pine nuts, salt and pepper to taste. Mix well. Pour mixture into a 3-quart glass baking dish. Cover and bake 1 hour. Uncover and bake 20 minutes. Serves 10.

Wild rice...a delectable Minnesota produce. Serve with a broccoli and tomato salad.

Zita 'n Meatballs Hot Dish

1 1/2 pounds ground beef

1 pound hot Italian link sausage, casings removed, crumbled

2 tablespoons minced yellow onions

2 cloves garlic, minced

1 10-ounce package frozen chopped spinach, thawed

1/2 cup plain dry bread crumbs

1 divided cup grated Parmesan cheese

2 eggs

1/2 teaspoon salt

1/4 teaspoon ground black pepper

6 cups prepared spaghetti sauce

8 ounces Mozzarella cheese, cut up

15 ounces Ricotta cheese

PREHEAT OVEN TO 375°F

In a bowl, combine beef, sausage, onions, garlic, spinach, bread crumbs, 1/2 cup Parmesan cheese, eggs, salt and pepper. Mix well and shape into 4 dozen meatballs. Pour spaghetti sauce into a deep saucepan; bring to a simmer, and place meatballs, into sauce. Cover and simmer 35 minutes. Cook zita according to package directions. Drain and place into a 4-quart baking dish. Add sauce and meatballs; stir. Cover with foil. Bake 25 minutes. Stir in Mozzarella cheese. In a bowl, combine Ricotta and remaining Parmesan cheese; drop by rounded tablespoonful over top. Cover and bake 15 minutes. Serves 12.

You can vary the amount of meatballs, by the size made. Serve this dish with a tossed salad.

PORK

Broccoli 'n Ham Hot Dish

- 1 4-ounce jar process cheese spread
- 1 10³/₄-ounce can condensed cream of chicken soup, undiluted
- ¹/₂ cup whole milk
- ¹/₂ cup chopped onions
- 2 tablespoons butter
- 1 10-ounce package frozen chopped broccoli
- 2 cups diced fully cooked ham
- 1 cup minute rice
- ¹/₄ teaspoon Worcestershire sauce

PREHEAT OVEN TO 350°F

In a large bowl, blend cheese, soup and milk. In a saucepan, stir and cook onion in butter until tender. Cook broccoli according to package directions until almost tender, but not done; drain. Add to soup mixture along with onions, ham, rice and Worcestershire sauce; mix well. Spoon mixture into two 1¹/₂-quart glass baking dishes. Cover tightly. Bake 1 hour. Serves 6.

This hot dish will freeze well. If frozen, bake uncovered one hour and thirty minutes.

Country Cassoulet

2 tablespoons butter

2 medium size onions, chopped

2 medium size carrots, chopped

1 pound Polish sausage, sliced

2 cloves garlic, minced

1/4 cup dry white wine or apple juice

1 cup chicken broth

1 8-ounce can tomato puree

1 teaspoon dried thyme leaves

1 teaspoon dried parsley

1/4 teaspoon dried oregano

1 cup cut-up cooked pork

1 cup cut-up cooked lamb

1 16-ounce can cannellini beans
rinsed and drained (white beans)

1/2 cup fresh bread crumbs mixed
with 2 tablespoons melted butter

PREHEAT OVEN TO 350°F

Melt butter in a large saucepan. Add onions, carrots and sausage; stir and cook 10 minutes. Stir in garlic, wine, broth, tomato puree, thyme, parsley, oregano, pork, and lamb. In a greased 2½-quart glass baking dish, layer half of the saucepan mixture, then top with half the beans; repeat. Sprinkle with bread crumbs. Bake about 40 minutes. Serves 8.

A hearty hot dish...serve with your favorite bread.

Effie's Chili Hot Dish

½ pound bulk pork sausage

½ pound ground beef

1 cup chopped onions

2 tablespoons chopped green bell pepper

3 cloves garlic, chopped

½ teaspoon salt

¼ teaspoon ground black pepper

1 8-ounce can tomato sauce

1 8-ounce can whole tomatoes, undrained, cut up

2 16-ounce cans pinto beans, drained

2 teaspoons chili powder

Pinch cayenne

2 teaspoons brown sugar

1 tablespoon white vinegar

2 teaspoons prepared mustard

PREHEAT OVEN TO 375°F

In a large saucepan, over medium heat, stir and cook pork sausage, ground beef, onion, bell pepper, garlic, salt and pepper until meat is done, about 10 minutes. Drain fat. Add tomato sauce and whole tomatoes; stir and cook 2 minutes. Stir in remaining ingredients; mix well. Pour mixture into a 2½-quart baking dish. Bake uncovered 45 minutes. Serves 6.

Serve this hot dish with a crisp salad and with warm corn muffins...buttered of course.

109

Ham 'n Corn Hot Dish

1 cup cubed fully cooked ham

1/2 cup chopped onions

1/2 cup chopped red bell pepper

1 16-ounce can creamed corn

1 10-ounce package whole kernel corn, thawed

1/2 cup whole milk

1 8-ounce package seasoned bread cubes

3 tablespoons butter, melted

1 tablespoon Worcestershire sauce

2 tablespoons grated Parmesan cheese

PREHEAT OVEN TO 350°F

In a bowl, combine first six ingredients; mix well. Spoon mixture into a buttered 2-quart glass baking dish. Top with bread cubes. In a small bowl, combine butter and Worcestershire sauce; spoon evenly over bread cubes. Bake uncovered 40 minutes. Sprinkle top with Parmesan cheese. Bake until melted. Serves 4.

Serve this hot dish with crisp green salad.

Ham 'n Noodles Hot Dish

1 8-ounce package medium noodles, cooked according to package directions, drained

2 cups cubed cooked ham

2 cups shredded Swiss cheese

1 10¾-ounce can condensed cream of celery soup, undiluted

1 cup dairy sour cream

½ cup chopped onions

½ cup chopped green bell pepper

PREHEAT OVEN TO 350°F

In a greased 13x9x2-inch baking dish, layer ⅓ of noodles, ham and cheese. In a bowl, combine soup, sour cream, onions, and green pepper; spread half the mixture over top. Repeat layers. Bake uncovered about 45 minutes or until very hot. Serves 6.

A green salad and rolls will complete this meal.

Ham-Potatoes Hot Dish

1 tablespoon butter

1/4 cup chopped green onions

1/4 cup chopped green bell pepper

4 medium size russet potatoes, thinly sliced in rounds

1 1/2 cups cubed cooked ham

1 10 3/4-ounce can cheddar cheese soup, undiluted

1/2 cup sour cream

1/2 cup whole milk

1/4 cup shredded cheddar cheese

Pinch ground black pepper

1 cup frozen peas & carrots, thawed

PREHEAT OVEN TO 350°F

In a saucepan, melt butter over medium heat. Add onions and green bell pepper. Stir and cook until soft; spoon into a large bowl. Add potatoes and ham. In a saucepan, over medium heat, combine soup, sour cream, milk, cheese, and black pepper; stir until cheese is melted. Add peas and carrots; stir and cook until bubbly. Pour over potato mixture; mix well. Spoon mixture into a 2-quart glass baking dish. Cover tightly. Bake 1 1/2 to 2 hours or until potatoes test done. Serves 4 to 6.

Simple and quick to prepare...serve this hot dish with sliced tomatoes and a crisp green salad, along with warm rolls.

Hue's Ham-Corn Hot Dish

3 tablespoons butter

3 tablespoons all-purpose flour

1 1/2 cups whole milk

3/4 teaspoon dry mustard

1/4 teaspoon ground black pepper

1/2 teaspoon Worcestershire sauce

1/2 cup finely chopped onions

1/2 cup finely diced green bell pepper

1 16 1/2-ounce can whole kernel corn

2 cups diced fully cooked ham

1/2 cup shredded sharp cheddar cheese

1/4 cup plain dry bread crumbs, mixed with 1 tablespoon melted butter

PREHEAT OVEN TO 350°F

In a large saucepan, melt butter over medium heat. Gradually stir in flour. Then gradually stir in milk; stir and cook mixture until smooth. Stir in remaining ingredients except bread crumbs; mix well. Spoon mixture into a 2-quart baking dish. Top with bread crumbs. Bake uncovered 40 minutes. Serves 6.

Serve this tasty hot dish with a lettuce, tomato and cucumber salad, along with warm crusty bread.

Italian Sausage Rice Hot Dish

- 1 10-ounce package chicken-flavor rice and pasta, prepared according to package directions, set aside
- 1 pound Italian sausage, casing removed
- 1/2 cup chopped onions
- 1 1/2 cups tender zucchini 1/4-inch slices
- 3 cloves garlic, minced
- 2 1/2 cups spaghetti sauce, divided
- 1/2 teaspoon dried basil
- 2 cups shredded Mozzarella cheese, divided

PREHEAT OVEN TO 350°F

In a large saucepan, crumble sausage. Add onions; stir and cook until sausage is browned; drain, reserving 1 tablespoon drippings in saucepan. Remove sausage and onions; set aside. Add zucchini and garlic; stir and cook over medium-high heat 1 minute. Cover and cook 2 minutes. In a bowl, mix together rice, sausage, onions, 1 1/2 cups spaghetti sauce and basil. Spoon into a 2 1/2-quart baking dish. Sprinkle with 1 cup cheese. Top with zucchini mixture. Top with remaining spaghetti sauce; sprinkle with remaining cheese. Bake about 30 minutes or until thoroughly heated. Serves 8.

Serve with a green salad tossed with Italian dressing and Parmesan cheese.

Macaroni Ham & Cheese

1¼ cups uncooked macaroni

5 tablespoons butter

½ cup chopped onion

¼ cup chopped green bell pepper

5 tablespoons all-purpose flour

½ teaspoon salt

¼ teaspoon black pepper

2 cups whole milk

8 ounces American or Swiss cheese, cut up

1¼ cups cubed or diced cooked ham

PREHEAT OVEN TO 375°F

Cook macaroni in salted water until just barely tender; drain and place into a 1½-quart glass baking dish. Melt butter in a heavy saucepan over medium heat. Add onion and green bell pepper; stir and cook until just tender but not brown. Gradually stir in flour; stir and cook until well blended. Add salt and pepper. Stir in milk. Bring to a boil, stirring constantly; boil 1 minute. Stir in cheese until melted. Stir in ham. Pour mixture over macaroni; stir well. Bake uncovered 35 minutes. Serves 6.

Serve with fresh sliced tomatoes and hard rolls.

Mary Dow's Ham & Cheese

12 slices white bread, crust removed

1½ cups shredded sharp cheddar cheese, divided

1 10-ounce package chopped broccoli, cooked and drained

1 cup cooked chopped ham

1 8-ounce package cream cheese, softened

3 eggs

1 cup whole milk

½ teaspoon dry mustard or 1 teaspoon prepared mustard

½ teaspoon salt

Pinch white pepper

PREHEAT OVEN TO 350°F

Place 6 slices of bread on bottom of a lightly buttered 11x7x2-inch glass baking dish. Layer with 1 cup cheddar cheese, then broccoli, and ham. Top with the remaining bread slices cut in half diagonally. In a bowl, combine cream cheese and eggs; mix until well blended. Stir in milk, mustard, salt and white pepper until blended; pour mixture over bread. Top with remaining cheddar cheese. Bake 50 minutes, or until set. Remove from oven; let stand 10 minutes before serving. Serves 6.

Make this special hot dish for the family...serve with a fresh fruit salad.

Pizza Hot Dish

- 1 11-ounce package refrigerated French bread loaf dough
- 1 8-ounce jar pizza sauce or 1 cup homemade
- 1 8-ounce package pepperoni slices
- 1/2 pound bulk pork sausage, cooked, drained
- 1 tablespoon olive oil
- 1/2 cup finely chopped onions
- 1 small green bell pepper, chopped
- 1 8-ounce package fresh mushrooms, sliced
- 1 3-ounce can sliced black olives, drained
- 1/4 cup grated Parmesan cheese
- 1 teaspoon pizza seasoning
- 2 cups shredded Mozzarella cheese

PREHEAT OVEN TO 400°F

Spread dough onto bottom and 1/2-inch up sides of a 13x9x2-inch baking dish, starting at the center. Spread enough pizza sauce to cover bottom of dough to desired taste; top with pepperoni and sausage. In a saucepan, heat olive oil. Add onions and bell pepper; stir and cook 2 minutes; top evenly over last layer. Add mushrooms to same saucepan; stir and cook 3 minutes; drain and top evenly over last layer. Top evenly with olives, Parmesan cheese, pizza seasoning and Mozzarella cheese. Bake uncovered 15 to 20 minutes or until cheese melts. Serves 6.

Invite the gang over for this pizza hot dish. Serve with tossed salad.

Pork & Beans Hot Dish

1 pound bulk pork sausage

1/2 cup chopped onions

1 cup sliced celery

2 cloves garlic, finely chopped

2 21-ounce cans baked beans in tomato sauce

1 16-ounce can lima beans, drained

1 16-ounce can kidney beans, drained

1 8-ounce can tomato sauce

2 teaspoons dry mustard

2 tablespoons brown sugar

1 tablespoon white vinegar

1 teaspoon salt

1/2 teaspoon Worcestershire sauce

Pinch cayenne pepper

PREHEAT OVEN TO 400°F

In a saucepan, stir and cook sausage, onions and celery 5 minutes. Add garlic; stir and cook until sausage is done, about 5 minutes; drain fat. Place mixture into a 3-quart baking dish. Add remaining ingredients; mix well. Bake uncovered 45 minutes or until hot and bubbly.

Serve with a shredded cabbage and carrot salad, along with crusty bread...buttered of course.

Pork 'n Beef Hot Dish

1 16-ounce can diced tomatoes, undrained

1 cup water

3 tablespoons quick-cooking tapioca

1 teaspoon granulated sugar

1¼ teaspoons salt

¼ teaspoon ground black pepper

1 tablespoon corn oil

1½ pounds beef stew meat, cut into bite-size chunks

½ pound pork, cut into bite-size

3 medium size russet potatoes, peeled and quartered

3 carrots, scraped and cut into chunks

2 stalks celery, cut into chunks

1 large onion, cut into chunks

3 cloves garlic, chopped

1 tablespoon dry bread crumbs

PREHEAT OVEN TO 375°F

In a large bowl, combine tomatoes, water, tapioca, sugar, salt and pepper. In a saucepan, heat corn oil. Add beef and pork; stir and cook until browned. Add to bowl. Add remaining ingredients to bowl; mix well. Pour mixture into a greased 13x9x2-inch glass baking dish. Cover and bake until meat is tender, about 2 hours. Serves 6.

This hot dish is like a stew. Serve in bowls along with crusty bread, or over hot cooked white rice along with green salad.

Pork Chops Hot Dish

2 tablespoons corn oil

4 1-inch thick pork chops

1¼ cups uncooked regular white rice

1 14½-ounce can diced tomatos

1 10½-ounce can beef consomme

1 1¾-ounce package dry onion soup mix

½ teaspoon thyme

½ teaspoon oregano

½ teaspoon salt or to taste

Pinch ground black pepper

PREHEAT OVEN TO 350°F

In a heavy saucepan, over medium heat, brown pork chops in corn oil. Place uncooked rice in a greased shallow 2-quart glass baking dish. Place pork chops on top of rice. In same saucepan, combine remaining ingredients; mix well. Pour mixture over chops. Cover and bake 1¼ hours. Serves 4.

A broccoli slaw will go well with this pork chop hot dish. Serve along with chunky applesauce.

Pork Chops with Sauerkraut

1 tablespoon corn oil

4 boneless pork chops, seasoned with salt and ground black pepper

1 cup chopped onions

1 16-ounce can sauerkraut, drained

1¼ cups water

¼ cup uncooked barley

¼ cup onion-flavor barbecue sauce

PREHEAT OVEN TO 350°F

Heat corn oil in a saucepan. Add pork chops and onions; brown lightly. Set pork chops aside. Place onions, sauerkraut, water and barley into a 2-quart rectangular glass baking dish; mix well. Top with pork chops. Spread barbecue sauce over pork chops. Cover with foil; bake 1½ hours or until pork is done. Serves 4.

Pork chops were a favorite of my husband's Uncle George. He didn't follow much of anyone's advice on what he should eat...he lived to be over 95!

Sausage Chili Hot Dish

1 tablespoon olive oil

1 cup chopped onions

2 cloves garlic, coarsely chopped

3/4 cup chopped green bell pepper

1 pound Italian sausage, crumbled

1 cup uncooked regular long grain white rice

1 16-ounce can kidney beans, drained

1 16-ounce can stewed tomatoes with jalapenos and spices, undrained, cut up

2 cups chicken broth

1/2 cup water

2 teaspoons chili powder

1/4 teaspoon ground cumin

1 cup shredded cheddar cheese

PREHEAT OVEN TO 375°F

In a large saucepan, heat oil. Add onions, garlic and bell pepper; stir and cook 1 minute. Add sausage. Stir and cook over medium heat until sausage is brown. Drain all but 1 tablespoon drippings. Place meat mixture into a large bowl. Add rice to saucepan; stir and cook 3 minutes; add to bowl. Add remaining ingredients except cheese to bowl. Mix well. Spoon mixture into a 13x9x2-inch glass baking dish. Cover with foil. Bake 1 hour. Remove foil; sprinkle top with cheese. Bake uncovered until cheese is melted. Serves 6 to 8.

All you need with this chili hot dish is green salad and freshly baked corn muffins.

Sausage Wild Rice Hot Dish

1 cup wild rice

1 pound bulk sausage

1 6-ounce can sliced mushrooms, drained

1 10³/₄-ounce can condensed cream of mushroom soup, undiluted

1 medium onion, thinly sliced

PREHEAT OVEN TO 350°F

In a saucepan, cook rice following package directions, until tender, but not mushy; drain. In another saucepan, stir and cook sausage until done; drain fat. Stir in mushrooms and soup. Add to rice; mix well. Spoon half the mixture into a buttered 2-quart glass baking dish. Top with onions. Spoon remaining mixture evenly over onions. Bake covered 1 hour. Serves 4.

This is a good hot dish to add to a brunch selection.

Sausage with Rigatoni

4 cups broccoli florets

1/4 pound hot Italian sausage, casing removed

1/2 cup finely chopped onions

1 26-ounce jar Marinara sauce

1 8-ounce package shredded part-skim Mozzarella cheese

2 tablespoons freshly grated Parmesan cheese

1 pound rigatoni, cooked according to package directions

PREHEAT OVEN TO 375°F

In a 4-quart saucepan, bring one inch of water to a boil. Add broccoli. Reduce heat to low; cover and simmer 2 minutes. Drain; set aside. In the same saucepan, break up sausage with a spoon. Add onion; cook and stir until well browned. Add Marinara sauce; stir until heated through. In a large bowl, mix all ingredients with cooked rigatoni. Spoon mixture into a shallow 2½-quart baking dish. Cover with foil. Bake 25 minutes or until bubbly and cheese is melted. Serves 6.

I like to make my own Marinara sauce...but the jarred sauce is so handy. Serve with a green salad.

Scalloped Potatoes & Ham

5 tablespoons butter, divided
1/4 cup all-purpose flour
3 cups whole milk
1 teaspoon dried parsley flakes
1 teaspoon salt
1/2 teaspoon dried thyme
1/4 teaspoon ground black pepper
6 cups thinly sliced peeled potatoes
1 1/2 cups chopped fully cooked ham
1 small onion grated

PREHEAT OVEN TO 375°F

In a saucepan, melt 4 tablespoons butter. Stir in flour. Gradually stir in milk. Stir in parsley, salt, thyme and black pepper. Bring to a boil; stir and cook 2 minutes. In a bowl, combine remaining ingredients; spoon half the mixture into a 2 1/2-quart baking dish. Top with half the sauce mixture. Repeat layers. Cover and bake about 70 minutes or until potatoes are almost done. Uncover; dot with remaining butter. Bake uncovered until potatoes are done, about 15 minutes. Serves 6.

This is an old favorite hot dish...always tasty. Serve with a crisp green salad and sliced fresh tomatoes.

Spam Hot Dish

1 12-ounce can spam luncheon meat

1/2 pound cheese, grated

3/4 cup cracker crumbs

1 10³/4-ounce can condensed cream of mushroom soup, undiluted

1 cup whole milk

3 eggs, well beaten

1 small onion, minced

1 small green bell pepper, minced

PREHEAT OVEN TO 350°F

In a large bowl, combine all ingredients; mix well. Pour mixture into a 2-quart baking dish. Bake 1 hour. Serves 4 to 6.

Spam originated in Minnesota. When it came on the store shelves, many dishes were created. This hot dish recipe dates back to the early '50s.

Spuds & Chops Hot Dish

4 medium size potatoes, peeled and quartered, boiled in lightly salted water until just tender, drained, set aside

4 thick pork chops, seasoned lightly with salt and pepper

1 tablespoon corn oil

1¹/₂ tablespoon butter

1 large onion, cut in rings

1¹/₂ tablespoons all-purpose flour

1 cup chicken or beef bouillon

1¹/₂ teaspoons vinegar

¹/₄ teaspoon garlic salt

Salt and black pepper to taste

1 cup dairy sour cream

PREHEAT OVEN TO 375°F

In a saucepan, over medium heat, brown pork chops in corn oil. Place into a shallow 2-quart glass baking dish. Place potatoes with chops. In same saucepan, melt butter. Add onion; stir and cook until soft. Remove onion and add to pork chops. In same butter, stir flour constantly for 2 minutes, do not let brown. Stir in bouillon, vinegar and garlic salt. Add salt and pepper to taste. Remove from heat. Stir in sour cream until blended. Pour mixture over all. Cover; bake 35 minutes. Uncover and bake 30 minutes. Serves 4.

A good hot dish to make for that special "meat and potatoes" person.

127

Vienna Sausage Hot Dish

1½ tablespoons corn oil

3 tablespoons chopped onions

2 tablespoons chopped green bell pepper

½ cup chopped celery

2 16-ounce cans pork and beans

2 teaspoons brown sugar

2 4-ounce cans Vienna sausage, drained

PREHEAT OVEN TO 350°F

In a saucepan, heat corn oil. Add onions and bell pepper; stir and cook until browned. Add celery; stir and cook 1 minute. Remove from heat. Stir in beans and sugar. Spoon mixture into a 2-quart glass baking dish. Place sausages on top. Bake until browned, about 30 minutes. Serves 6.

This recipe dates back to the '50s...serve with a shredded cabbage salad, tossed with a vinegar-and-oil type dressing.

Zucchini-Sausage Rice Hot Dish

1 10-ounce package chicken flavor rice and pasta mix, prepared according to package directions, set aside

1 pound Italian sausage, casing removed

1/2 cup chopped onions

3 small zucchini, cut into 1/4-inch slices

2 cloves garlic, minced

2 1/2 cups spaghetti sauce, divided

1/2 teaspoon dried basil

2 cups shredded Mozzarella cheese, divided

PREHEAT OVEN TO 350°F

In a large saucepan, crumble sausage. Add onions; stir and cook until sausage is browned; drain, reserving 1 tablespoon drippings in saucepan. Remove sausage and onions; set aside. Add zucchini and garlic; stir and cook over medium-high heat 1 minute. Cover and simmer 2 minutes. In a bowl, mix together rice, sausage, onions, 1 1/2 cups spaghetti sauce and dried basil; spoon into a 2 1/2-quart glass baking dish. Sprinkle with 1 cup cheese. Top with zucchini mixture. Top with remaining spaghetti sauce, and sprinkle with remaining cheese. Bake about 30 minutes or until thoroughly heated. Serves 8.

Serve with a green salad tossed with an Italian-type dressing and grated Parmesan cheese.

SEAFOOD

Almond Crab Hot Dish

- 1 10³/₄-ounce can condensed cream mushroom soup, undiluted
- 1 cup chopped celery
- ¼ cup chopped onions
- 1 3-ounce can chow mein noodles
- 1 8-ounce can sliced water chestnuts, drained
- 1 4-ounce can mushroom pieces
- 1 teaspoon Worcestershire sauce
- 1 6-ounce package frozen crabmeat, thawed, liquid reserved
- 6 tablespoons toasted slivered almonds

PREHEAT OVEN TO 350°F

In a bowl stir together soup, celery, onions, noodles, water chestnuts, mushrooms and Worcestershire sauce. Fold in crabmeat and reserved liquid. Spoon into a greased 1½-quart baking dish. Top evenly with almonds. Bake about 30 minutes or until hot and bubbly. Serves 4.

Serve with a crisp green salad, along with rolls.

Cheesy Fish Rice & Asparagus

2 cups cooked regular long grain white rice

1 pound fresh, tender asparagus, spears cut into 1-inch pieces, blanched 1 minute, drained

2 pounds orange roughy fillets, cut into serving portions

3 tablespoons butter

1 medium size onion, chopped

1 clove garlic, minced

5 tablespoons all-purpose flour

1 cup whole milk

1/4 teaspoon salt

1/4 teaspoon white pepper

1 cup shredded cheddar cheese

3/4 cup unseasoned dry bread crumbs mixed with 5 tablespoons grated Parmesan cheese

PREHEAT OVEN TO 350°F

In a lightly greased 13x9x2-inch glass baking dish, spoon rice evenly onto bottom. Top evenly with asparagus. Place fish fillets over asparagus. In a saucepan, over medium heat, add butter and onions; stir and cook 2 minutes; do not brown. Add garlic; stir and cook a few seconds. Gradually stir in flour until blended. Add milk gradually, stirring constantly, until slightly thickened. Stir in salt, pepper and cheddar cheese until melted; pour mixture top. Sprinkle with bread crumbs. Cover; bake 35 minutes. Uncover; bake 10 minutes. Serves 4.

Serve a crisp salad and rolls to complete this meal.

Chopstick Tuna Hot Dish

½ 10¾-ounce can condensed cream of mushroom soup, undiluted

½ cup skim milk

¼ cup water

1 7-ounce can tuna, drained

1 10-ounce package frozen peas

1 8-ounce can sliced water chestnuts, undrained

1 medium size tomato, peeled and diced

½ cup chopped celery

5 tablespoons sliced green onions

2 tablespoons light soy sauce

1½ ounces chow mein noodles, divided

PREHEAT OVEN TO 375°F

In a bowl, combine soup, milk and water; stir to blend. Add tuna; mix well. Add remaining ingredients except reserve half the noodles. Mix lightly. Spoon mixture into a lightly greased 1½-quart glass baking dish. Top with remaining noodles. Bake 25 to 30 minutes, until very hot. Serves 6.

When looking for yet another way to prepare tuna...try this oriental-style hot dish.

Crab-Tomatoes Hot Dish

- 1 10-ounce package wide egg noodles, cooked according to package directions 5 minutes, drained
- 2 tablespoons butter
- 1/4 cup sliced green onions
- 1/2 teaspoon salt
- 1/4 teaspoon ground black pepper
- 2 tablespoons all-purpose flour
- 1 cup whole milk
- 1 teaspoon Dijon mustard
- 1 teaspoon Worcestershire sauce
- 1 cup shredded cheddar cheese
- 1 15-ounce can tomato sauce with tomato bits
- 2 6-ounce cans crabmeat, drained, or imitation crabmeat
- 2 tablespoons plain dry bread crumbs
- 2 tablespoons Parmesan cheese

PREHEAT OVEN TO 350°F

In a saucepan, melt butter. Add green onions, salt, black pepper and flour; stir and cook 1 minute. Stir in milk, mustard and Worcestershire sauce; bring to a boil, stirring often. Remove from heat; stir in cheese until melted. Stir in tomato sauce and crabmeat. Place noodles into a 2-quart baking dish. Gently stir sauce into noodles. In a small bowl, combine bread crumbs and grated Parmesan cheese; sprinkle over noodles. Bake uncovered 25 to 30 minutes. Serves 4.

You can use fresh crabmeat in this dish, if desired. Serve with green salad and rolls.

Doris's Tuna Hot Dish

1½ cups whole milk

1 8-ounce package cream cheese, cut up

1 10-ounce package frozen peas, cooked, drained

7 ounces spaghetti cooked according to package directions, drained

1 9-ounce can tuna, drained, flaked

1 5-ounce can mushrooms, drained

¼ cup grated Parmesan cheese

1 tablespoon chopped pimiento

1 tablespoon chopped onions

½ teaspoon onion salt

¼ teaspoon oregano leaves, crushed

Pinch ground black pepper

PREHEAT OVEN TO 350°F

In a saucepan, heat milk and cream cheese over low heat; stir until smooth. Add remaining ingredients; mix well. Pour mixture into a 2-quart baking dish. Bake 25 minutes. Serves 6.

Cousin Doris lives on a beautiful Minnesota lake, but will often serve tuna as well as walleye!

Favorite Tuna Hot Dish

- 1 7-ounce package elbow macaroni cooked 3 minutes less than package directions, drain
- 1 9-ounce can solid tuna, drained
- 1 8-ounce can small peas, drained
- 1 tablespoon minced onions
- 1 10³/4-ounce can condensed cream of mushroom soup, undiluted
- 1¹/2 cups whole milk
- 1¹/4 cups crushed potato chips, divided

PREHEAT OVEN TO 350°F

In a 2-quart buttered glass baking dish, combine macaroni, tuna, peas, onions and ¹/2 cup potato chips. In a saucepan, over medium heat, bring soup and milk to a boil, stirring constantly; pour mixture over all. Sprinkle with remaining potato chips on top. Bake uncovered about 35 minutes or until hot. Serves 4.

My husband's Aunt Mollie served this tuna hot dish to me when I first came to Minnesota as a bride. She served it with a molded lime gelatin salad. I serve it with a mixed greens salad...both good.

Fish 'n Potato Hot Dish

4 medium size potatoes, peeled, boiled until almost tender, drained and sliced 1/8-inch thick

1 teaspoon all-purpose flour

1 small onion, sliced into rings

1/4 teaspoon ground black pepper

3/4 cup milk

1 1/2 pounds cod fillets

1 tablespoon grated Parmesan cheese

2 tablespoons minced fresh parsley

1/4 teaspoon paprika

PREHEAT OVEN TO 375°F

Place potatoes into a greased 2-quart shallow baking dish. Sprinkle with flour. Top with onion rings. Sprinkle with black pepper. Pour half the milk over potatoes. Place fish on top; pour remaining milk over fish. Sprinkle with Parmesan cheese. Cover and bake until fish flakes, about 25 minutes. Remove from oven; sprinkle with parsley and paprika. Serves 4.

Minnesotans loves cod. We serve it in many ways. Some folks have a traditional Christmas dish called lutefisk...served with drawn butter if you are Norwegian...cream sauce if you are Swedish. This hot dish is another way of serving cod fish.

Fish Sticks Au Gratin

3 medium size potatoes,
  very thinly sliced

2 tablespoons all-purpose flour

4 tablespoons butter

  Salt and black pepper to taste

1 1/2 cups grated cheddar cheese

1 cup whole milk, heated

1 10-ounce package frozen fish sticks

In a 2-quart glass baking dish, layer potato slices, 1 tablespoon flour, 2 tablespoons butter, salt and pepper, 1/2 cup cheese and 1/2 cup hot milk. Repeat layers. Place fish on top. Sprinkle with remaining cheese. Bake covered 20 minutes. Remove cover; bake 20 minutes. Serves 4.

This is a hot dish most kids will like. Serve with peas and carrot along with warm rolls.

Friday's Fish & Shrimp

1 cup chopped onions

1 tablespoon olive oil

3 cloves garlic, finely chopped

1 28-ounce can stewed tomatoes, including juice

1/2 cup water

Salt to taste

Ground black pepper to taste

3 tablespoons chopped fresh parsley

1/4 teaspoon dried oregano, crushed

1 pound cod or haddock, boned

1/2 pound cleaned fresh shrimp

6 ounces feta cheese, cut into chunks

Hot cooked rice or orzo pasta

PREHEAT OVEN TO 400°F

In a saucepan, stir and cook onions in olive oil over medium heat until tender. Add garlic; stir and cook a few seconds. Add tomatoes, water, salt, pepper, parsley and oregano. Bring to a boil, then reduce heat. Cover; simmer 15 minutes, stirring often. Spoon sauce into a 2½-quart glass baking dish. Arrange fish on top. Cover and bake 15 minutes. Add shrimp and feta cheese. Cover and bake 15 minutes. Serve over hot cooked rice or hot cooked orzo pasta. Serves 6.

A tossed salad will go well with this dish.

Hearty Shrimp Hot Dish

- 1 tablespoon olive oil
- 1 cup chopped onions
- 3 cloves garlic, thinly sliced
- 1 medium size green bell pepper, chopped
- 2 19-ounce cannellini beans, drained and rinsed
- 1 15-ounce can tomatoes, diced
- 1 cup low sodium chicken broth
- 1/2 teaspoon salt, or to taste
  Pinch ground black pepper
- 1/4 teaspoon dried basil
- 1/4 teaspoon dried thyme
- 1/2 cup Kalamata olives, pitted and halved
- 1 pound cleaned fresh shrimp
- 1/2 dry bread crumbs, mixed with 1/4 cup Parmesan cheese

PREHEAT OVEN TO 400°F

In a large saucepan, add oil, onions, garlic and bell pepper; stir and cook over medium heat until tender, about 4 minutes. Add beans, tomatoes, broth, salt, pepper, basil, thyme and olives. Bring to a slow boil. Reduce heat. Add shrimp, and simmer 4 minutes. Spoon mixture into a 3-quart baking dish. Sprinkle top with bread crumbs. Bake uncovered 25 minutes or until bubbly and very hot. Serves 8.

This shrimp hot dish is much like a cassoulet.

Herbed Rice 'n Fish Hot Dish

- 1 teaspoon chicken bouillon granules, mixed in 1½ cups boiling water
- ½ cup uncooked regular white rice
- ¼ teaspoon Italian seasoning
- ¼ teaspoon garlic powder
- 1 10-ounce package frozen chopped broccoli, thawed, drained
- 1 2.8-ounce can French fried onions, divided
- 1 tablespoon grated Parmesan cheese
- 1 pound unbreaded fish fillets, fresh or frozen, thawed if frozen
- ½ cup shredded cheddar cheese

PREHEAT OVEN TO 400°F

In an 11x7x2-inch shallow baking dish, combine hot bouillon, rice and seasonings. Bake covered 10 minutes. Top with broccoli, half the onions and Parmesan cheese. Place fish diagonally down center of dish. Bake covered about 25 minutes or until fish flakes easily with a fork. Gently stir rice. Top fish with shredded cheddar cheese and remaining onions. Bake uncovered 3 minutes or until onions are golden brown. Serves 4.

Serve with a tossed salad and hard rolls.

Oyster Wild Rice

- 2 cups soft bread crumbs, mixed with 1/2 cup melted butter
- 1/2 cup wild rice, cooked according to package directions
- 1 cup raw oysters, liquor reserved
- 2 tablespoons butter, cut up

  Chicken broth, canned

  Oyster liquor from raw oysters

PREHEAT OVEN TO 350°F

In a buttered 1 1/2-quart glass baking dish, layer half of the buttered bread crumbs, half the rice, and all the oysters. Dot with butter, and top with remaining rice. Add enough chicken broth to the oyster liquor to measure 1 1/2 cups; pour over rice. Sprinkle top with remaining buttered bread crumbs. Cover with foil. Bake 30 minutes. Remove foil; bake 15 minutes or until crumbs are golden. Serves 4.

A simple hot dish to make for special friends.

Nelan's Seafood Hot Dish

5 tablespoons butter

1 large size onion, chopped

1 tablespoon chopped garlic

1/2 cup chopped green bell pepper

1/4 cup chopped fresh parsley

3/4 cup regular uncooked long grain white rice

1 103/4-ounce can condensed cream of mushroom soup, mixed with 3/4 cup milk

2 cups cleaned fresh shrimp

11/2 cups fresh crab meat, picked over

1/2 teaspoon salt, or to taste

1/4 teaspoon ground black pepper

1/2 cup unseasoned dry bread crumbs, mixed with 1 tablespoon melted butter

PREHEAT OVEN TO 350°F

In a saucepan, over medium heat, melt butter. Add onion, garlic, bell pepper and parsley; stir and cook until soft but not brown. Add rice and soup; stir until thoroughly heated. Add shrimp, crab meat, salt and pepper; stir to mix. Pour mixture into a 21/2-quart glass baking dish. Cover and bake 10 minutes. Sprinkle top with bread crumbs; bake about 35 minutes or until rice is tender. Serves 6.

Salad and crusty bread will complete this tasty meal.

Norse Fish Hot Dish

3 tablespoons butter

3 tablespoons all-purpose flour, mixed with 1/4 teaspoon salt and pinch ground black pepper

1 1/4 cups whole milk

2 eggs, separated

1 teaspoon ground nutmeg, optional

1 pound cod fillets, cut into cubes

1 cup elbow macaroni, cooked a little less time than package direction

4 slices American cheese, cut into strips

5 tablespoons dry bread crumbs

5 tablespoons melted butter, mixed with 2 teaspoons lemon juice and 2 tablespoons minced fresh parsley, kept warm

PREHEAT OVEN TO 350°F

In a saucepan, melt butter. Stir in flour mixture. Stir in milk until smooth; cook and stir over low heat until thickened, about 7 minutes. Beat egg yolks, and stir into sauce. Stir in nutmeg. In a large bowl, combine white sauce, fish and macaroni. In a bowl, beat egg whites until stiff; fold into bowl mixture. Pour mixture into a 1 1/2-quart baking dish. Place cheese over top. Sprinkle with bread crumbs. Bake 30 minutes. When serving, top with warm butter mixture. Serves 4.

Fish and Minnesota...goes together like cod and Norse!

Parmesan Shrimp Hot Dish

- 1 14-ounce package bow tie pasta, cooked according to package directions, drained, set aside
- 6 tablespoons butter
- 3 cloves garlic, finely chopped
- 2 tablespoons minced onion
- 6 tablespoons all-purpose flour
- 2½ cups half & half (light cream)
- ¾ cup clam juice
- 1 tablespoon catsup
- ½ teaspoon salt
- ¼ teaspoon white pepper
- 1 tablespoon minced fresh dill
- 1 pound peeled uncooked shrimp
- ¾ cup Parmesan cheese, divided

PREHEAT OVEN TO 350°F

In a saucepan, melt butter over medium heat. Add garlic and onion; stir and cook 1 minute. Stir in flour to make a white roux, do not brown. Gradually stir in half & half. Add clam juice, catsup, salt, pepper, dill and 5 tablespoons Parmesan cheese; stir until well blended. Place pasta and shrimp into a lightly buttered 2-quart glass baking dish. Add sauce mixture; stir to mix well. Sprinkle remaining cheese on top. Bake uncovered about 40 minutes or until bubbly. Serves 6.

This is a good hot dish for company. Serve with French bread and a crisp green salad.

Salmon Rice Hot Dish

1 cup long grain regular white rice, cooked in salted water 15 minutes, drained if needed

1 tablespoon fresh lemon juice

1/4 cup chopped fresh parsley

4 tablespoons butter, divided

1 pound salmon fillet, cut into 2-inch pieces

1 1/2 pounds fresh asparagus, cut in half crosswise, blanched

1/2 cup finely chopped onions

3 tablespoons all-purpose flour

1 1/2 cups chicken stock or broth

1/2 cup heavy cream

1/4 teaspoon salt

Pinch ground black pepper

1/2 cup Parmesan cheese, divided

PREHEAT OVEN TO 450°F

In a bowl, mix together, rice, lemon juice, parsley and 1 tablespoon butter. Spoon mixture into a shallow 2-quart glass baking dish. Place salmon on top of rice. Place asparagus on top of salmon. In a saucepan, stir and cook onions in remaining butter until tender. Gradually stir in flour until well blended. Add stock; stir until thickened. Stir in cream, salt, black pepper and 4 tablespoons cheese. Pour sauce over all. Sprinkle with remaining cheese. Bake about 25 minutes or until very hot and top is brown. Serves 4.

A pretty hot dish...garnish with sliced tomatoes.

Salmon with Saffron Rice

- 1 cup chopped onions
- 2 tablespoons olive oil
- 4 cloves garlic, chopped
- 1/4 teaspoon dried thyme, crushed
- 5 cups cooked rice (rice salted when cooked)
- 1 teaspoon saffron threads, crushed and soaked in 5 tablespoons boiling water
- 2 tablespoons butter
- 1 pound skinless salmon fillet, cut into 4 portions, lightly seasoned with salt and ground black pepper

  Parsley sprigs for garnish

PREHEAT OVEN TO 350°F

In a saucepan, stir and cook onions in olive oil until golden, about 5 minutes. Add garlic; stir and cook a few seconds. Place mixture into a bowl. Stir in thyme. Stir in rice and saffron mixture; set aside. Melt butter in the same saucepan. Fry salmon, over medium heat, 2 minutes on each side. Spoon half the rice mixture into a greased 2-quart glass baking dish. Place salmon over rice. Spoon the remaining rice mixture over salmon. Cover and bake 40 minutes. Garnish with parsley when serving. Serves 4.

Serve with a lettuce and tomato salad tossed with an Italian dressing, along with buttered peas.

Sam's Fresh Seafood Lasagne

7 tablespoons butter

7 tablespoons all-purpose flour

3 cloves garlic, minced

1/2 teaspoon salt

1/4 teaspoon black pepper

2 cups chicken broth

2 cups whole milk

1/2 cup thinly sliced green onions, including tops

13/4 cups shredded Mozzarella cheese

1 3-ounce package cream cheese

9 uncooked lasagne noodles

1 cup creamed cottage cheese

1 cup cooked minced fresh clams or one 7-ounce can minced clams, drained

1 cup fresh crab meat, picked over

1 cup cooked fresh shrimp, cut up

1/2 cup grated Parmesan cheese

PREHEAT OVEN TO 350°F

In a large saucepan, melt butter. Stir in flour and garlic; cook, stirring constantly, until blended. Stir in salt, pepper, broth and milk. Bring to a boil; stir and cook 1 minute. Add onions, Mozzarella and cream cheese; stir and cook until melted. Spread 1 1/2 cups cheese sauce evenly into a 13x9x2-inch glass baking dish. Top with 3 uncooked noodles; spread with cottage cheese. Repeat with 1 1/2 cups cheese sauce, 3 uncooked noodles. Top with clams, crabmeat, shrimp and 1 1/2 cups cheese sauce. Top with remaining noodles, sauce and Parmesan cheese. Bake uncovered until noodles test done, about 40 minutes. Serves 10.

Serve a crisp green salad with this special hot dish. Like Sam...unforgettable.

Scallops 'n Shrimp Hot Dish

- 3/4 cup small fresh scallops, liquid reserved
- 2 eggs, slightly beaten
- 2 cups cooked regular long grain white rice
- 3/4 cup cut up boiled fresh shrimp
- 2 tablespoons diced onions
- 2 tablespoons butter
- 1/4 cup tomato catsup
- 1/2 teaspoon celery salt
- 3/4 teaspoon curry powder

PREHEAT OVEN TO 350°F

In a bowl, combine liquid from scallops with eggs; add rice, scallops and shrimp. In a small saucepan, brown onions lightly in butter. Add catsup, celery salt and curry powder; stir into rice mixture. Place mixture into a 1 1/2-quart shallow baking dish. Bake 30 minutes or until firm. Serves 6.

Serve with a crisp green salad and French bread.

Seafood Hot Dish

2 tablespoons butter

1 8-ounce package fresh button mushrooms, sliced

2 1/2 cups cut up cooked fresh shrimp

1/2 cup fresh crab meat, picked

1/2 teaspoon salt

1/4 teaspoon ground black pepper

1 tablespoon Worcestershire sauce

2 1/2 cups thinly sliced celery

3/4 cup thinly sliced onions

1/2 cup chopped green bell pepper

4 hard-boiled eggs, chopped

1 1/2 cups mayonnaise–not salad dressing

1 8-ounce can sliced water chestnuts, drained

3/4 cup unseasoned dry bread crumbs, mixed with 1/4 cup grated Parmesan cheese

1/2 cup slivered almonds

PREHEAT OVEN TO 350°F

In a saucepan, melt butter over medium heat. Add mushrooms; stir and cook 5 minutes. Place into a large bowl. Add remaining ingredients except bread crumbs and almonds. Mix gently to blend well. Spoon mixture into a greased 2 1/2-quart baking dish. Sprinkle with bread crumbs and almonds. Bake 40 minutes or until hot and bubbly. Serves 8.

Serve this seafood hot dish with a green salad, tossed with an Italian dressing, along with rolls.

Seafood-Noodle Hot Dish

2 tablespoons margarine

2 pounds flounder or other fish fillets cut into 1-inch pieces

1 3½-ounce can French fried onions

4 cups medium size noodles, cooked and drained

1 4-ounce can sliced mushrooms, drained

¼ cup chopped pimientos

2 10¾-ounce cans condensed cheddar cheese soup, undiluted

1 cup whole milk

1 teaspoon salt

1 teaspoon paprika

1 teaspoon Worcestershire sauce

PREHEAT OVEN TO 350°F

In a saucepan, melt margarine over medium heat. Add fish; cook on both sides until firm. Place into a large bowl. Reserve ½ cup onions for topping. Add remaining onions, noodles, mushrooms and pimientos to bowl. In a saucepan, combine soup, milk and seasonings; heat and stir until smooth. Pour over fish mixture; stir carefully. Pour mixture into a shallow 11x7x2-inch baking dish. Bake 30 minutes or until hot and bubbles around the edges. Sprinkle reserved onions on top 5 minutes before end of baking time. Serves 6.

Serve with a garden salad along with warm bread.

Seafood Stuffed Manicotti

2 tablespoons butter

1 medium size onion, chopped

1/4 cup finely chopped parsley

1 stalk celery, finely chopped

1 16-ounce can tomatoes, undrained, cut up

1 cup chicken broth

1/2 teaspoon dried basil

Pinch white pepper

3/4 pound fresh crab meat, cooked

1/2 pound fresh medium size shrimp cooked, and quartered

3 thinly sliced green onions, including green tops

1 cup shredded Fontina cheese

8 large manicotti shells, uncooked

1 10-ounce container refrigerated reduced-fat Alfredo sauce

1/4 cup grated Parmesan cheese

PREHEAT OVEN TO 375°F

In a saucepan, melt butter over medium heat. Add chopped onions; stir and cook until tender. Stir in parsley, celery, tomatoes, broth, basil, and white pepper. Simmer 30 minutes. In a bowl, combine crab, shrimp, green onions and Fontina cheese; set aside. Cook manicotti in salted water until almost tender, but still firm; rinse with cold water, and drain well. Spread enough tomato sauce to cover bottom of a 13x9x2-inch glass baking dish. Stuff cooked manicotti with seafood mixture; place side by side over tomato sauce, and pour more sauce on sides of manicotti but not on top. Pour the Alfredo sauce over center of manicotti. Sprinkle top with Parmesan cheese. Bake uncovered 25 minutes. Serves 4.

A salad of mixed greens will compliment this special seafood pasta hot dish.

Shrimp and Ham Hot Dish

1½ cups elbow macaroni, cooked 6 minutes in salted water, drained

2 strips bacon, diced

½ cup chopped onions

½ cup chopped green bell pepper

1 clove garlic, chopped

1 20-ounce can tomatoes, undrained, cut up

½ teaspoon salt

1 cup fresh, cooked, cleaned shrimp

½ pound cubed cooked ham

½ cup dry bread crumbs, mixed with 2 tablespoons grated Parmesan cheese and 2 tablespoons melted butter

PREHEAT OVEN TO 350°F

In a saucepan, over medium heat, stir and cook bacon until crisp; drain half the drippings. Add onions, green pepper and garlic to same saucepan; stir and cook until tender. Add tomatoes and salt; stir until well heated. Add shrimp, ham and macaroni; mix well. Pour mixture into a 1½-quart glass baking dish. Top with bread crumb mixture. Bake, uncovered, 30 minutes, until very hot. Serves 4.

This hot dish has a creole flavor...serve with a crisp green salad and crusty rolls.

Shrimp and Rice Hot Dish

4 cups chicken broth
  Pinch crushed saffron
3 tablespoons olive oil
1 medium onion, finely chopped
2 tablespoons finely chopped green
  bell pepper
2 cloves garlic, finely chopped
2 cups uncooked regular white rice
  Salt and black pepper to taste
2 cups peeled raw shrimp, cut into
  1/2-inch pieces
1/2 cup diced cooked smoked sausage

PREHEAT OVEN TO 400°F

Heat broth in a saucepan; stir in saffron; set aside. Heat olive oil in a saucepan over medium-high heat. Add onions and bell pepper; stir and cook 5 minutes. Add garlic; stir and cook a few seconds. Add rice; stir and cook 1 minute. Add salt and pepper to taste. Stir in broth mixture. Add shrimp and sausage; stir to mix well. Pour mixture into a lightly greased shallow 2-quart glass baking dish. Bake 40 minutes or until rice test done. Serves 4.

Almost paella...serve with a crisp green salad.

Shrimp-Shrimp Hot Dish

- 8 ounces egg noodles, cooked according to package directions, less 3 minutes cooking time, drain
- 2 10-ounce cans cream of shrimp soup
- 1½ cups whole milk
- 1 cup mayonnaise, not salad dressing
- ¼ cup diced celery
- 2 tablespoons diced yellow onions
- ½ teaspoon salt
  Pinch ground black pepper
- 10 tablespoons shredded cheddar cheese
- 2 cups fresh shrimp, cut up
- ¼ cup chow mein noodles

PREHEAT OVEN TO 350°F

In a bowl, combine all ingredients except chow mein noodles; mix well. Pour mixture into a 2-quart baking dish. Bake uncovered 35 minutes. Top with chow mein noodles; bake 10 minutes. Serves 8.

A double-shrimp hot dish...use frozen shrimp, thawed, if fresh are unavailable.

Tuna Broccoli Hot Dish

2 7-ounce cans tuna, drained and flaked

1½ cups cooked regular white rice

1 10-ounce package frozen chopped broccoli, cooked, drained

½ cup chopped onion

2 tablespoons chopped pimiento

½ teaspoon salt

Pinch ground black pepper

1 8-ounce package cream cheese, cubed

¼ cup whole milk

¼ cup grated Parmesan cheese

Fresh parsley sprigs

PREHEAT OVEN TO 350°F

In a large bowl, combine tuna, rice, broccoli, onion, pimiento, salt and pepper. In a saucepan, over low heat, stir cream cheese and milk until smooth. Stir in Parmesan cheese. Add to tuna mixture. Mix well. Spoon mixture into an 10x6-inch baking dish. Bake 40 minutes. Garnish with parsley when serving, as desired. Serves 6 to 8.

Cream cheese makes this tuna hot dish special.

Tuna Broccoli Brie Hot Dish

- 8 ounces penne pasta
- 1 large broccoli stalk, coarsely chopped, cooked in water 5 minutes, drained
- 1 small onion, minced
- 6 ounces Brie cheese, rind removed
- 1 1/2 cups whole milk
- 1/2 teaspoon Dijon mustard
- 4 green onions, sliced
- 1/2 cup diced roasted red pepper
- 1 9-ounce can solid white water-packed tuna, drained, flaked
- 1/2 teaspoon salt
- 1/4 teaspoon freshly ground black pepper
- 1 fresh tomato, seeded, diced

PREHEAT OVEN TO 350°F

In a saucepan, cook pasta according to package directions; drain. Add cooked broccoli. Add onion and cheese, stirring gently until cheese melts. Add milk and mustard; stir to blend. Add remaining ingredients except plum tomato; stir. Place mixture into a buttered 2-quart baking dish. Bake about 30 minutes or until hot and bubbly. Stir in diced tomato just before serving. Serves 4.

Serve this special tuna hot dish with a salad and crusty bread.

Tuna-Mushroom Hot Dish

- 1 12-ounce package wide noodles, cooked, drained
- 2 7-ounce cans tuna, drained
- 1 4-ounce can mushroom stems and pieces, drained
- 1 tablespoon grated onion
- 1 10³/4-ounce can condensed cream of mushroom soup, undiluted
- 1¹/4 cups whole milk
- ¹/2 teaspoon salt
- ¹/4 teaspoon black pepper
- ¹/2 cup crushed saltine crackers, mixed with 3 tablespoons melted butter
- Paprika, optional

PREHEAT OVEN TO 350°F

In a large bowl, combine noodles, tuna, mushrooms and onions In a saucepan, over medium heat, combine soup, milk, salt and pepper; stir until just heated. Pour over noodle mixture; mix well. Pour into a lightly greased 11¹/2x7¹/2x2-inch glass baking dish. Sprinkle top with cracker crumbs. Bake, uncovered 35 to 45 minutes or until thoroughly heated. Serves 6.

A simple, but tasty hot dish. Serve with sliced fresh tomatoes and cucumbers, along with hard rolls.

Tuna Noodle Hot Dish

3³/4 cups wide egg noodles, cooked according to package directions, drained (6-ounces)

1 10³/4-ounce can condensed cream of mushroom soup, undiluted

1¹/4 cups whole milk

6 tablespoons grated Parmesan or Romano cheese

¹/4 cup chopped pimiento-stuffed olives

1 tablespoon minced yellow onion

¹/4 teaspoon garlic powder

1 9¹/4-ounce can tuna, drained, flaked

Salt to taste

Ground black pepper to taste

PREHEAT OVEN TO 350°F

In a bowl, combine all ingredients except cooked noodles; stir to mix well. Stir in cooked noodles. Spoon mixture into a lightly buttered 2-quart baking dish. Bake uncovered about 30 minutes or until hot, bubbly and lightly browned. Serves 4.

Tuna and noodles...a popular hot dish. Serve with a lettuce and tomato salad, tossed with an Italian-type salad dressing.

Tuna-Rice Hot Dish

1 tablespoon butter

1/2 cup chopped onions

2 cups cooked rice

1 7-ounce can tuna in oil, flaked

1 1/2 cups milk

3 eggs, beaten

1/4 teaspoon salt

Pinch black pepper

PREHEAT OVEN TO 350°F

In a saucepan, over medium heat, melt butter. Add onions; stir and cook until tender. In a bowl, combine all ingredients. Spoon into a buttered 2 1/2-quart glass baking dish. Place baking dish in a baking pan filled with 1-inch of water. Bake 45 minutes. Serves 6.

This hot dish recipe dates back to the early 50's. Serve with a lettuce and tomato salad and rolls.

Tuna Rotini Hot Dish

2 cloves garlic, minced

2 eggs, slightly beaten

1/4 teaspoon salt

1/2 cup Alfredo sauce, homemade or purchased

4 cups cooked rotini pasta, cooked according to package directions

1 9-ounce can light chunk tuna, drained

1 1/2 cup fresh chopped broccoli, or 1 10-ounce package frozen chopped broccoli, thawed

1 cup seasoned croutons

2 tablespoons Parmesan cheese

PREHEAT OVEN TO 350°F

In a bowl, mix together garlic, eggs, salt, and Alfredo sauce until blended. Stir in cooked rotini, tuna, and broccoli. Pour mixture into a shallow 2-quart glass baking dish. Bake covered, about 25 minutes or until mixture is set. Remove from oven; top with croutons, and sprinkle with cheese. Serves 6.

Serve this hot dish with a molded strawberry-fruit gelatin salad, along with hard rolls.

EGGS

Asparagus Ham and Eggs

1½ pounds fresh asparagus, cut into 2-inch pieces

3 tablespoons butter, melted

1 1-pound loaf sliced bread, crusts removed

¾ cup shredded cheddar cheese, divided

2 cups cubed cooked ham

6 eggs

3 cups whole milk

2 teaspoons dried minced onion

½ teaspoon salt

¼ teaspoon dry mustard

Pinch ground black pepper

PREHEAT OVEN TO 325°F

In a saucepan, cover asparagus with water. Cover and cook until just tender but still a little firm; drain. Brush butter lightly on one side of bread slices. Place half of the bread, buttered side up, into a greased 13x9x2-inch glass baking dish. Sprinkle with ½ cup cheese. Layer with asparagus and ham. Top with remaining bread, buttered side up. In a bowl, beat eggs lightly. Add milk, onion, salt, mustard and pepper. Pour over bread. Cover and refrigerate overnight. Remove from refrigerator 20 minutes before baking. Bake, uncovered 50 minutes. Sprinkle with remaining cheese. Bake until cheese is melted, and a knife inserted near center comes out clean. Serves 10.

This hot dish is made for brunch. Serve with breads, muffins, fresh fruit and juice.

Breakfast Burritos Hot Dish

8 strips bacon

8 large fresh mushrooms, sliced

6 green onions, sliced

6 tablespoons chopped green bell pepper

2 cloves garlic, chopped

8 large eggs

1/4 cup dairy sour cream

1 cup shredded cheddar cheese

3 tablespoons taco sauce

1 tablespoon butter

4 9-inch flour tortillas

PREHEAT OVEN TO 350°F

In a saucepan, cook bacon until crisp; remove, crumble and set aside. Drain all but 1 tablespoon drippings. Add mushrooms, onions, green pepper and garlic to saucepan. Stir and cook until tender; remove and set aside. In a bowl, beat eggs and sour cream. Stir in 1/4 cup cheese and taco sauce. In same saucepan, melt butter; add egg mixture. Cook stirring until eggs are set. Add bacon and mushroom mixture. Spoon down center of tortillas; roll up. Place seam-side down in an 11x7x2-inch baking dish. Sprinkle with remaining cheese. Bake until cheese melts, about 5 minutes. Serves 4.

Top this dish with more sour cream when serving.

Chilaquile Hot Dish

1 tablespoon corn oil

1 cup chopped onions

1 teaspoon minced garlic

12 corn tortillas, torn into 1-inch pieces

2 cups shredded Monterey Jack cheese

2 4½-ounce cans chopped mild green chilies

4 large eggs

2 cups buttermilk

½ teaspoon salt

¼ teaspoon ground black pepper

⅛ teaspoon cumin

⅛ teaspoon dried oregano

PREHEAT OVEN TO 350°F

Heat corn oil in a saucepan, over medium-low heat. Add onions and garlic; stir and cook 5 minutes. Spread half the tortillas onto bottom of an 11½x7½x2-inch greased glass baking dish. Sprinkle half the cheese and 1 can chilies over top. Sprinkle onion mixture over chilies. Repeat layering remaining tortillas, cheese and chilies. In a medium bowl, whisk together remaining ingredients. Pour over all. Bake about 45 minutes, until set and browned on top. Serves 6.

This dish is a good way to use up leftover tortillas. Serve for lunch or a light supper. A crisp green salad will complete the meal.

Cinnamon French Toast

2 cups whole milk

1/4 teaspoon vanilla extract

3 eggs, lightly beaten

12 slices whole wheat bread, cut in half cross-wise

2 tablespoons butter, melted

1/2 cup powdered sugar

11/2 cups golden raisins

21/2 teaspoons ground cinnamon

PREHEAT OVEN TO 400°F

In a medium bowl, combine milk, vanilla and eggs; whisk until blended. Dip bread into mixture to coat. In a buttered 9x9-inch square glass baking dish, layer 1/3 of the bread onto bottom; drizzle evenly with 1/3 butter, sprinkle with 21/2 tablespoons sugar; sprinkle with half the raisins. Repeat layer, going a different direction with the bread. Top with remaining bread, butter and sugar. Sprinkle top evenly with ground cinnamon. Cover and bake 25 minutes. Remove cover; bake 15 minutes. Serves 6.

Tempt the teenagers with this breakfast dish.

Egg Hot Dish

1½ cups sliced celery

1 cup chopped green bell pepper

1 medium size onion, thinly sliced

2 tablespoons butter

1½ tablespoons all-purpose flour

1 teaspoon salt

1 16-ounce can whole tomatoes, undrained, cut up

¼ teaspoon hot pepper sauce

6 hard boiled eggs, chopped

2 cups hot cooked regular white rice, cooked without salt

½ cup shredded American cheese

PREHEAT OVEN TO 350°F

In a large saucepan, over medium heat, stir and cook celery, green pepper and onions in butter until tender. Add flour and salt, stir until blended. Stir in tomatoes and hot pepper sauce; bring to a boil. Reduce heat, and simmer uncovered 10 minutes or until thickened and bubbly, stirring occasionally. Gently stir in chopped eggs. Spoon rice onto bottom of a 2-quart greased glass baking dish. Pour egg mixture over rice. Bake uncovered 25 to 30 minutes or until thoroughly heated. Top with cheese during the last 5 minutes of baking time. Serves 6.

A meatless hot dish...serve with fresh asparagus for lunch or a light supper.

Egg and Sausage Hot Dish

8 ounces sweet or hot Italian sausage, casings removed, crumbled

2 teaspoons olive oil

2 cups red bell pepper strips

2 medium onions, thinly sliced

1 teaspoon salt, divided

4 large eggs

5 cups whole milk

Pinch ground black pepper

1 1-pound loaf Italian bread, sliced 1/2-inch thick and quartered

1 cup shredded Fontina cheese

PREHEAT OVEN TO 350°F

In a saucepan, stir and cook sausage until browned; drain and set aside. Add oil to same saucepan. Add peppers, onions and 1/4 teaspoon salt. Stir and cook 15 minutes. In a bowl, beat eggs, milk, remaining salt and black pepper. Place enough bread to cover bottom of a 13x9x2-inch glass baking dish. Spread half the pepper and onion mixture over bread; top with half the sausage; sprinkle with half the cheese. Pour half the milk mixture over all. Repeat, starting with bread. Cover with plastic wrap; refrigerate overnight. Remove from refrigerator 1 hour before baking. Discard plastic wrap. Cover with foil; bake 30 minutes. Uncover; bake 25 minutes. Serves 8.

A good egg dish to fix ahead of time for a brunch.

Helen's Ham & Eggs

12 slices white bread,

1 pound fully cooked ham, diced

2 cups shredded cheddar cheese

6 large eggs

3 cups whole milk

2 teaspoons Worcestershire sauce

3/4 teaspoon dry mustard

1/2 teaspoon salt, or to taste

1/4 teaspoon ground black pepper

Pinch cayenne ground pepper

1 small yellow onion, finely chopped

3 tablespoons chopped green
bell pepper

1 tablespoon, chopped red
bell pepper

1/4 cup butter, melted

1 cup crushed cornflakes

PREHEAT OVEN TO 350°F

Remove crust from bread; place 6 slices on bottom of a greased 13x9x2-inch baking dish. Top evenly with ham and cheese. Top with remaining bread. In a bowl, beat eggs; add remaining ingredients except butter and cornflakes. Pour mixture over all. Cover and refrigerate 8 hours. Remove cover; spoon butter evenly over top. Sprinkle evenly with cornflakes. Bake uncovered about 1 hour or until a knife inserted near center comes out clean. Remove from oven; let stand a few minutes before serving. Serves 8.

A tasty hot dish for brunch or supper...serve with fresh fruit along with cinnamon-apple muffins.

Hilda's Favorite Chile Rellenos

1 cup chopped onions

1½ tablespoons butter

2 5-ounce cans chopped green chilies, drained

2 cups shredded cheddar cheese

1 cup shredded hot pepper Monterey Jack cheese

3 eggs

1 cup dairy sour cream

¼ teaspoon salt

¼ teaspoon crushed red pepper flakes

1 cup chopped seeded fresh tomatoes

PREHEAT OVEN TO 350°F

In a saucepan, stir and cook onions in butter until tender. Stir in green chilies; spoon evenly into a greased 8x8-inch square baking dish. Sprinkle with cheeses. In a bowl, beat eggs lightly. Add sour cream, salt and pepper flakes; beat until blended. Spoon mixture over cheese. Sprinkle with chopped tomatoes. Bake about 40 minutes or until a knife inserted in center comes out clean. Serves 6.

Hilda has a passion for Mexican food. She serves this dish with a fresh fruit salad and warm bread.

Overnight Ham 'n Eggs

6 slices bread

2 tablespoons butter, softened

2 cups shredded cheddar cheese

3/4 pound cooked ham, thinly sliced

1 8-ounce package fresh mushrooms, sliced and sauteed in 1 tablespoon butter

1 7-ounce can diced green chilies

2 cups shredded Monterey Jack cheese

6 eggs

2 cups whole milk

1 1/2 teaspoons salt

1/2 teaspoon paprika

1/2 teaspoon dry mustard

1/4 teaspoon ground black pepper

1/4 teaspoon onion salt

1/4 teaspoon dried basil

PREHEAT OVEN TO 350°F

Spread bread with butter on one side only; place buttered-side down into a 13x9x2-inch glass baking dish. Sprinkle with cheddar cheese. Layer ham on top of cheese, then the mushrooms, and chilies. Top with Monterey Jack cheese. In a medium bowl, beat eggs. Add remaining ingredients; stir until blended. Pour mixture over all. Cover with plastic wrap; refrigerate overnight. Remove from refrigerator 1 hour before baking. Remove plastic wrap. Bake uncovered 50 minutes. Let stand 10 minutes before serving. Serves 6.

A hearty egg hot dish...perfect to serve for a late family breakfast with toast and fresh fruit juice.

Sam's Burritos

1 large green bell pepper, chopped

3/4 cup chopped onions

2 tablespoons butter

8 eggs, lightly beaten with a pinch salt and a pinch ground black pepper

1/2 cup shredded cheddar cheese

1/2 cup shredded Jack cheese

1 1/2 cups picante sauce

8 8-inch flour tortillas

Dairy sour cream

PREHEAT OVEN TO 350°F

In a saucepan, stir and cook bell pepper and onions in butter until tender but not brown. In a bowl, mix together eggs and cheeses. Add to saucepan; stir and cook until eggs are set and cheese is melted. Remove from heat. In a small saucepan, heat picante sauce; dip each tortilla into sauce one at a time. Spoon 1/2 cup egg mixture onto center of each tortilla. Fold 2 sides over egg mixture; fold ends under, and place into a 13x9x2-inch glass baking dish. Top with remaining picante sauce. Bake about 10 minutes or until very hot. Remove from oven. Top with sour cream as desired when serving. Serves 8.

When Sam first tasted a flour tortilla, he said it reminded him of lefse...a bit thicker, but something he could get use to...and enjoys serving this burrito hot dish for brunch along with assorted fresh fruit.

Sausage 'n Eggs Hot Dish

- 1 pound breakfast sausage packaged in a roll
- 1 8-ounce refrigerated crescent dinner rolls
- 2 cups shredded Mozzarella cheese
- 4 eggs, beaten
- 3/4 cup whole milk
- 3/4 teaspoon salt
  Pinch ground black pepper

PREHEAT OVEN TO 425°F

In a saucepan, crumble sausage. Stir and cook over medium heat until completely done; drain well. Line bottom of a buttered 13x9x2-inch glass baking dish with crescent rolls, firmly pressing perforations to seal. Sprinkle with sausage and cheese. In a bowl, combine remaining ingredients; beat well, and pour over all. Bake about 15 minutes or until set. Remove from oven; let stand 5 minutes. Cut into serving-size squares; serve immediately. Serves 6.

This is an easy hot dish to make for a quick and special breakfast or brunch.

Scrambled Eggs 'n Broccoli

4 tablespoons butter, divided

1/4 cup all-purpose flour

2 cups whole milk

2 cups shredded cheddar cheese

1 cup sliced fresh mushrooms

1/4 cup finely chopped onions

12 eggs, beaten

1 teaspoon salt

1 10-ounce package frozen chopped broccoli, cooked and drained

1 cup soft bread crumbs, tossed with 1 tablespoon melted butter

PREHEAT OVEN TO 350°F

In a saucepan, melt 2 tablespoons butter. Add flour; stir and cook until mixture begins to bubble. Gradually stir in milk. Bring to a boil; stir and cook 2 minutes. Remove from heat. Stir in cheese until melted. In a large saucepan, melt remaining butter. Add mushrooms and onions; stir and cook until tender. Add eggs and salt; stir and cook until eggs are completely set. Add cheese sauce and cooked broccoli; mix well. Pour mixture into a greased 11 1/2x7 1/2x2-inch glass baking dish. Sprinkle top with bread crumbs. Cover and refrigerate overnight. Remove from refrigerator 30 minutes before baking. Remove cover; bake uncovered 30 minutes. Serves 6.

This make ahead egg dish is perfect for a lazy morning breakfast. Serve with fruit juice along with biscuits or buttered toast.

Spuds Ham Eggs Hot Dish

1 2-pound bag frozen hash brown potatoes, not thawed

2 cups diced cooked ham

2 cups shredded Swiss cheese

1½ tablespoons butter

1 large red bell pepper, cut into ½-inch strips

1 8-ounce package fresh mushrooms, sliced

6 large eggs, slightly beaten

½ cup whole milk

1 cup small curd creamed cottage cheese

¼ teaspoon ground black pepper

PREHEAT OVEN TO 350°F

Layer half the potatoes into a 13x9x2-inch greased glass baking dish. Top with ham and cheese. In a saucepan, over medium heat, melt butter. Add bell pepper and mushrooms; stir and cook 5 minutes or until tender. Spoon over ham, cheese layer; top with remaining potatoes. In a bowl, combine eggs, milk, cottage cheese and black pepper; beat until well blended. Pour mixture over all. Bake uncovered about 50 minutes or until light brown and center is set. Serves 8.

A good hot dish for brunch or a light supper...serve with warm muffins, quick breads and fresh fruit.

Tangy Ham 'n Eggs

2 1-pound loaves Italian-style bread, cut into 1-inch cubes

6 cups cubed fully cooked ham

1½ pounds Monterey Jack cheese, cubed

1 medium onion, chopped

¼ cup butter

16 eggs, beaten

7 cups whole milk

½ cup prepared mustard

½ teaspoon Worcestershire sauce

Chopped fresh parsley

PREHEAT OVEN TO 350°F

In a large bowl, mix together bread, ham and cheese; place equal amounts of mixture into two lightly greased 13x9x2-inch glass baking dish. In a saucepan, stir and cook onions in butter until just tender. Place into a large bowl; add remaining ingredients to bowl and mix well. Pour equal amounts over each bread mixture. Cover and refrigerate at least 8 hours. Remove from refrigerator 30 minutes before baking. Bake, uncovered, 55 to 65 minutes or until a knife inserted near the center comes out clean. Remove from oven, garnish with parsley, and serve. Serves 24.

An egg hot dish perfect for brunch...serve with fresh fruit, juice and assorted warm muffins.

The Girls
Ham 'n Eggs

3 cups frozen shredded hashbrown potatoes

3/4 cup shredded Monterey Jack cheese

1 cup diced cooked ham

1/4 cup chopped green onions including tops

4 eggs

1 12-ounce can evaporated milk

1/4 teaspoon ground black pepper

Pinch salt

PREHEAT OVEN TO 350°F

Place potatoes into an 8-inch square glass baking dish. Sprinkle with cheese, ham and onions. In a bowl, beat together eggs, milk, pepper and salt. Pour over all. Cover and refrigerate for several hours. Remove from refrigerator 30 minutes before baking. Remove cover; bake uncovered 55 to 60 minutes or until a knife inserted near center comes out clean. Serves 6.

This is the egg hot dish the girls will purr for. You can refrigerate it overnight and bake it the next day. Serve with toast and strawberry jam.

SIDE DISHES

Baked Corn Dish

1 tablespoon butter

4 tablespoons margarine

1/2 cup chopped onions

1/2 cup chopped green bell pepper

4 tablespoons all-purpose flour

1 1/2 cups whole milk

2 teaspoons granulated sugar

2 eggs slightly beaten

2 16-ounce cans whole corn, drained

1/2 cup diced cooked ham

1/2 teaspoon salt, or to taste

1/8 teaspoon black pepper

PREHEAT OVEN TO 350°F

In a saucepan, over medium heat, melt butter. Add onions and bell pepper; stir and cook until tender. Remove and set aside. To same saucepan, add margarine. Blend in flour, stirring constantly 3 minutes. Remove from heat. Gradually stir in milk. Add sugar. Return to medium heat; bring to a boil, stirring constantly; boil 1 minute. Quickly stir in egg. Add remaining ingredients. Mix well. Pour mixture into a 2 1/2-quart baking dish. Bake 40 minutes. Serves 8.

A tasty side dish to serve with most meats.

Baked Macaroni Primavera

8 ounces macaroni or penne pasta

1 tablespoon olive oil

6 tablespoons chopped green onions

3 cloves chopped garlic

1 medium size red bell pepper, chopped

1 tablespoon chopped fresh basil

1/2 teaspoon dried oregano

1/4 teaspoon ground cumin

1/2 cup asparagus tips, cut into 2-inch lengths

1 cup halved cherry tomatoes

1/2 cup snow peas, trimmed

2 teaspoons butter

2 teaspoons all-purpose flour

1 cup milk

1/2 cup grated Parmesan cheese

1/2 teaspoon ground black pepper

PREHEAT OVEN TO 400°F

In a large deep saucepan, boil macaroni in 2 quarts salted water until firm-tender; drain and return to saucepan; keep warm. In another saucepan, heat olive oil. Add green onions, garlic and bell pepper; stir and cook until soft, but not brown. Add basil, oregano, cumin, asparagus, tomatoes and snow peas; stir and cook 2 minutes. Remove from heat; place in saucepan with pasta. In a small saucepan, melt butter over medium heat. Stir in flour; stir and cook 2 minutes. Gradually add milk, whisking until sauce thickens. Remove from heat; stir in grated cheese and black pepper. Add to pasta mixture; toss. Spoon mixture into a greased 2 1/2-quart baking dish. Bake uncovered 25 minutes or until lightly brown and bubbly. Serves 4.

Serve this pasta as a side dish or a light lunch along with salad and warm bread.

Baked Noodles Romanoff

- 1 cup grated Parmesan cheese, divided
- 1 8-ounce package egg noodles or linguine, broken into thirds, cooked following package directions, drained
- 2 cups cottage cheese
- 1 cup dairy sour cream
- 1 small onion, finely chopped
- 2 teaspoons Worcestershire sauce
- 1 teaspoon paprika
- 1/2 teaspoon salt

  Few drops of hot red pepper sauce

PREHEAT OVEN TO 350°F

In a greased 2-quart baking dish, combine half the Parmesan cheese and remaining ingredients; mix well. Bake 30 minutes. Sprinkle top with remaining cheese; bake 5 minutes. Serves 6.

Serve as a special side dish or as a light lunch, along with a crisp green salad and French bread.

Baked Wild Rice

1 tablespoon butter

1/2 cup chopped onions

1 6-ounce package pure wild rice

1/4 teaspoon garlic powder

2 teaspoons Worcestershire sauce

1 tablespoon minced fresh parsley

1 3/4 cups chicken broth

1/2 cup dry wine, or apple juice

1 cup cubed sharp cheddar cheese

PREHEAT OVEN TO 350°F

Melt butter in a saucepan. Add onions; stir and cook until tender, about 4 minutes. Stir in rice; stir and cook until golden. Add garlic powder, Worcestershire sauce, parsley, chicken broth and wine. Bring to a boil. Stir in cheese. Spoon mixture into a buttered 1 1/2-quart baking dish. Bake covered 2 hours or until rice is tender. Serves 6.

Genuine wild rice is a familiar sight in parts of Minnesota...a great grain to use in many recipes, including this side dish.

Barley and Fruit Hot Dish

- ½ cup slivered almonds
- 2 tablespoons pine nuts
- 2 tablespoons butter
- 2 tablespoons margarine
- 2 cups pearl barley
- 1 cup sliced green onions
- 7 cups chicken broth
- ½ cup diced dried apricots
- ½ cup golden raisins
- 1 tablespoon crasins (dried cranberries)

PREHEAT OVEN TO 325°F

In a large saucepan, saute almonds and pine nuts in butter until light brown; place into a small bowl. In the same saucepan, add margarine, barley and onions; stir and cook until onions are soft but not brown. Add chicken broth; bring to a boil. Add apricots, raisins, crasins, almonds and pine nuts; stir well. Pour mixture into a greased 13x9x2-inch glass baking dish. Bake uncovered until barley is tender, about 1 hour and 20 minutes. Serves 8.

This is a good side dish to serve with baked ham.

Broccoli Rice Hot Dish

1½ tablespoons butter

½ cup chopped onions

½ cup chopped celery

1 10-ounce package frozen chopped broccoli, thawed

1 10¾-ounce can condensed cream of mushroom soup, undiluted

1 8-ounce jar process cheese spread

3 cups cooked long grain white rice

PREHEAT OVEN TO 325°F

In a large saucepan, over medium heat, melt butter. Add onions and celery; stir and cook 2 minutes. Add broccoli; stir and cook 3 minutes. Stir in soup, milk and cheese until blended. Spoon rice into a greased 8x8-inch square glass baking dish. Pour hot soup mixture evenly over top. Do not stir. Bake uncovered 30 minutes or until heated through and is bubbly. Serves 8.

Serve this good side dish with baked ham or with most any other meat.

Candied Sweet Potatoes

- 2 16-ounce cans dry-packed sweet potatoes
- 1/2 cup packed brown sugar
- 1 cup fresh orange juice
- 1/2 teaspoon freshly grated orange peel
- 1/2 teaspoon ground cinnamon
- 1/4 teaspoon ground nutmeg
- 2 tablespoons butter
- 1 teaspoon vanilla extract

PREHEAT OVEN TO 350°F

Place sweet potatoes into a shallow 1 1/2-quart baking dish. Combine remaining ingredients except vanilla in a saucepan; bring to a boil, stirring constantly; stir and boil 3 minutes. Stir in vanilla. Pour hot mixture over potatoes. Bake about 1 hour, basting often to glaze well. Serves 6.

For an extra treat top this side dish with chopped pecans and coconut the last 10 minutes baking time.

Cheesy Chili Rice Hot Dish

- 1 5-ounce package salsa-style rice mix
- 1½ cups shredded Mexican-style cheese blend, divided
- 1 15-ounce can chili beans in sauce, undrained
- 1 14½-ounce can diced tomatoes, undrained
- 1 tablespoon minced yellow onion
- ½ cup water

PREHEAT OVEN TO 425°F

Combine rice mix and ½ cup cheese in a lightly greased 1½-quart baking dish. In a saucepan, combine beans, tomatoes, onions and water. Bring to a boil; pour mixture over rice mixture, and stir until well mixed. Cover and bake 20 minutes or until rice is tender. Sprinkle with remaining cheese. Bake uncovered until cheese melts. Serves 4.

Serve this hot dish as a side dish or a complete meal when served with salad.

Cheesy Garlic Mashed Spuds

2 pounds russet potatoes, peeled and cut into pieces

6 large cloves garlic, peeled

2 tablespoons butter, softened

1/2 teaspoon salt

3/4 cup whole milk, heated

1 tablespoon chopped fresh chives

Pinch ground black pepper

1 1/2 cups shredded cheddar cheese, divided

Chopped fresh parsley

PREHEAT OVEN TO 350°F

In a saucepan, cover potatoes with water. Add garlic and salt. Cover and cook until potatoes are tender; drain. Add butter; mash well. Stir in milk, chives black pepper and half the cheddar cheese until blended. Spoon mixture into a buttered 2-quart baking dish. Sprinkle with remaining cheese on top. Cover and bake 30 minutes. When serving, garnish with chopped parsley as desired. Serves 8.

Lots of garlic in this potato side dish...yummy.

Company Mashed Potatoes

5 pounds Idaho potatoes, peeled, quartered

1 8-ounce package cream cheese, cut up

1 cup dairy sour cream

1/2 teaspoons salt or to taste

1/4 teaspoon ground black pepper

1/4 teaspoon onion salt

1/4 teaspoon garlic salt

2 tablespoons butter, cut up

Paprika

PREHEAT OVEN TO 350°F

In a large saucepan, boil potatoes in lightly salted water until tender; drain. In a large mixer bowl, add potatoes and cream cheese; mash with a hand masher. Add remaining ingredients; beat with an electric mixer until light and fluffy. Spoon mixture into a greased 2-quart glass baking dish. Bake uncovered 30 minutes. Sprinkle lightly with paprika; place under broiler a few seconds. Serves 8.

You can prepare this dish one day ahead of time. Cover and refrigerate. Remove from refrigerator 30 minutes before baking. Uncover dish and bake as above or until heated through.

Corn Hot Dish

- 6 tablespoon butter
- 1/2 cup finely chopped onions
- 1/2 cup chopped green bell pepper
- 1 16-ounce can whole kernel corn, undrained
- 1 16-ounce can cream corn
- 1 8-ounce package corn muffin mix
- 3 eggs, lightly beaten
- 1 cup dairy sour cream
- 2 slices bacon, crisply cooked, drained and crumbled
- 1 cup shredded cheddar cheese

PREHEAT OVEN TO 350°F

In a saucepan, melt butter over medium heat. Add onions and bell pepper; stir and cook until tender but not brown; place into a large bowl along with remaining ingredients. Mix well. Pour mixture into a 3-quart baking dish. Bake 50 minutes. Serves 8.

A tasty corn side dish...serve warm.

Corn Pudding

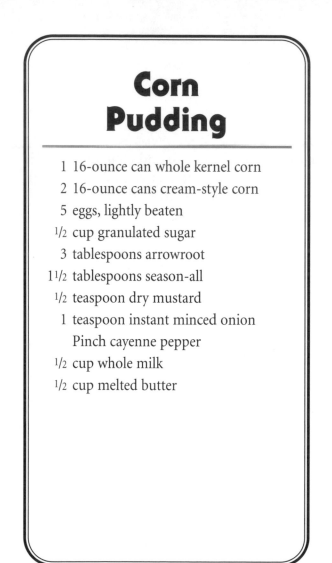

1 16-ounce can whole kernel corn

2 16-ounce cans cream-style corn

5 eggs, lightly beaten

1/2 cup granulated sugar

3 tablespoons arrowroot

1 1/2 tablespoons season-all

1/2 teaspoon dry mustard

1 teaspoon instant minced onion

Pinch cayenne pepper

1/2 cup whole milk

1/2 cup melted butter

PREHEAT OVEN TO 400°F

In a bowl, mix together corn and eggs. In another bowl, combine dry ingredients; stir into corn mixture. Add milk and butter; mix well. Pour mixture into a buttered 2 1/2-quart baking dish. Bake uncovered 1 hour or until knife comes out clean when inserted in center, stirring once after 30 minutes of cooking. Serve immediately. Serves 8.

Corn pudding...a tasty corn hot dish.

Country Corn Hot Dish

1 8-ounce package cream cheese, softened

2 eggs

1 12-ounce can whole kernel corn, drained

1 medium carrot, peeled, shredded

1/4 cup chopped green onions

1/4 cup chopped green bell pepper

1/4 teaspoon salt

Pinch ground black pepper

PREHEAT OVEN TO 350°F

In a bowl, combine cream cheese and eggs until well blended. Add remaining ingredients; mix well. Pour mixture into a lightly greased 8-inch square baking dish. Bake 40 minutes. Serves 4.

For added color, add 1 tablespoon chopped pimiento to mixture before baking, if desired.

Dilled-Scalloped Potatoes

3 large or 5 medium potatoes, peeled, thinly sliced in rounds

1 medium onion, chopped

3 tablespoons all-purpose flour

1½ tablespoons butter

1½ cups whole milk

½ teaspoon salt

Pinch ground black pepper

½ teaspoon dried dillweed

PREHEAT OVEN TO 350°F

In a 2-quart greased baking dish, layer ¼ of potatoes on bottom. Sprinkle with ⅓ onions. Sprinkle evenly with 1 tablespoon flour, and dot with 1 teaspoon butter. Repeat layers twice (totaling 3 layers each). Then top with the last layer of potatoes and dot with butter (no flour on this layer). Heat milk in a saucepan with salt, pepper and dillweed, until bubbles forms at the edge. Pour gently into baking dish. Cover and bake 30 minutes. Remove cover; press down on top layer with a large spoon to get liquid to rise to cover. Bake uncovered about 1 hour until potatoes are tender and top is lightly browned. Serves 6.

Scalloped potatoes are a favorite with Minnesotans.

Green Bean Hot Dish

- 1 10¾-ounce can condensed cream of mushroom soup, undiluted
- ¾ cup whole milk
  Pinch ground black pepper
- 2 9-ounce packages frozen cut green beans, thawed, or 2 14½-ounce cans cut green beans, drained
- 1½ cups canned French fried onions, divided

PREHEAT OVEN TO 350°F

Combine soup, milk and black pepper in a 1½-quart baking dish; mix well. Stir in green beans and half the French fried onions. Bake about 30 minutes or until very hot. Stir; sprinkle with remaining onions. Bake until golden, about 5 minutes. Serves 6.

This is the original green bean casserole, uffda, hot dish recipe...I found it on a can!.

193

Mushroom Cheese Lasagne

9 curly-edge lasagne noodles, cooked tender-firm, rinsed, drained

4 1/2 tablespoons butter, divided

1 pound fresh mushrooms, sliced

1/2 cup dry white wine

2 large cloves garlic, minced

1/4 cup all-purpose flour

4 cups whole milk

1 teaspoon salt

1/4 teaspoon cracked black pepper

1/4 teaspoon freshly grated nutmeg

Pinch cayenne pepper

1 1/2 cups grated Provolone cheese

1 1/2 cup grated Parmesan cheese

4 ounces cream cheese, cut up

1/2 teaspoon paprika

PREHEAT OVEN TO 350°F

Melt 1 1/2 tablespoons butter in a saucepan. Add mushrooms; stir and cook until light brown. Then add wine; cook until evaporated. In a saucepan, melt remaining butter. Add garlic; stir and cook 1 minute. Add flour; stir constantly 2 minutes. Add half the milk; stir until thickened. Add remaining milk, salt, pepper, nutmeg and cayenne; stir 5 minutes. Combine grated cheeses; stir in half, plus cream cheese, until melted. Place 3 noodles into a buttered 13x9x2-inch baking glass dish. Layer with half the mushrooms, 1/3 sauce. Repeat layer with remaining mushrooms and 1/3 sauce. Repeat layer with remaining sauce. Sprinkle top with remaining cheese and paprika. Bake 35 minutes. Let rest 15 minutes; cut. Serves 8.

For variation, add 1 cup cooked crab meat to sauce. Serve this creamy meatless lasagne with salad.

Potato-Apple Bake

- 2 teaspoons butter, melted
- 2 cups heavy or whipping cream
- 1 teaspoon salt
- 1/4 teaspoon freshly ground black pepper
- Pinch ground nutmeg
- 1/4 pound Fontina or Gouda cheese shredded
- 1 large Granny Smith apple, peeled, shredded
- 3 pounds baking potatoes, peeled

PREHEAT OVEN TO 350°F

Place melted butter into a 13x9x2-inch baking dish; spread over all. In a bowl, combine cream, salt, black pepper, nutmeg, cheese and shredded apple. Slice potatoes 1/8-inch thick; stir into cream mixture. Pour into buttered baking dish. Cover with foil. Bake 45 minutes. Remove foil; bake 35 minutes or until top is golden and potatoes are tender. Serves 16.

This is a good side dish to add to a buffet.

Potatoes with Red Peppers

3 tablespoons butter

1 cup chopped onions

3 tablespoons all-purpose flour

1/4 teaspoon salt

1/4 teaspoon ground black pepper

2 cups whole milk

1 cup shredded Swiss cheese

2 tablespoons minced fresh parsley

6 medium potatoes, peeled, thinly sliced

1 7-ounce jar roasted red sweet peppers, drained, coarsely chopped

Fresh parsley sprigs

PREHEAT OVEN TO 350°F

In a saucepan, over medium heat, melt butter. Add onions; stir and cook until soft but not brown. Stir in flour, salt and pepper. Gradually stir in milk; stir and cook until thickened and is bubbly. Remove from heat. Stir in cheese and minced parsley. Place half of the potatoes into an 11x7x2-inch glass baking dish. Cover with half the sauce and all of the red peppers. Repeat layers of potatoes and sauce. Cover with foil. Bake 1 hour and 15 minutes. Uncover; bake 15 minutes or until potatoes are tender. Garnish with parsley sprigs when serving. Serves 6.

When asked to bring a hot dish for potluck, but not a main dish, try this scalloped potatoes with roasted red peppers side dish...very nice.

Quick Bean Hot Dish

1/2 cup unsulphured molasses

3 tablespoons white vinegar

3 tablespoons prepared mustard

1/2 teaspoon liquid pepper sauce

3 16-ounce cans baked beans in tomato sauce

1 16-ounce can kidney beans, drained

1/2 pound frankfurters, cut into 1-inch pieces

1 cup diced cooked ham

3/4 cup chopped onions, divided

PREHEAT OVEN TO 375°F

In a bowl, mix together molasses, vinegar, mustard and pepper sauce; spoon into a 3-quart baking dish. Add beans, frankfurters, ham and half the onions; stir to mix well. Bake 1 hour. Just before serving, sprinkle remaining chopped onions on top of beans around edge of dish. Serves 10.

Serve as a side dish, or serve along with a salad and rolls for a complete meal.

Rice-Broccoli Hot Dish

2 cups cooked rice

1 8-ounce jar process cheese spread

1 10³/₄-ounce can condensed cream of chicken soup, undiluted

1 10-ounce package frozen chopped broccoli

Crushed potato chips

PREHEAT OVEN TO 375°F

In a bowl, stir all ingredients, except potato chips, until mixed. Spoon mixture into a 1¹/₂-quart baking dish. Sprinkle top with enough potato chips to cover. Bake uncovered about 35 minutes or until hot and bubbly. Serves 4.

For variation, top this side dish with crushed soda crackers mixed with chopped almonds.

Savory French-Cut Potato Bake

1/4 cup all-purpose flour

1/2 teaspoon salt

Pinch ground black pepper

1 1/2 cups whole milk

1 10 3/4-ounce condensed cream of celery soup, undiluted

1/2 pound process American cheese, cut up

6 large russet baking potatoes, cut into 4x1/2x1/2-inch pieces

1 large onion, chopped

1 tablespoon butter, cut up

Paprika

PREHEAT OVEN TO 350°F

In a saucepan, combine flour, salt and black pepper. Gradually stir in milk until smooth. Bring to a boil; stir and cook 2 minutes. Add soup; mix until blended and is heated. Add cheese; stir until smooth. Place potatoes into a buttered 13x9x2-inch baking dish. Top evenly with chopped onions and butter. Pour cheese sauce over all. Bake uncovered about 1 hour or until potatoes test done. Sprinkle lightly with paprika. Serves 6.

A creamy potato side dish with a different look.

Savory Party Potatoes

3 slices bacon

1/2 cup chopped onions

1/2 cup chopped green bell pepper

1 8-ounce package cream cheese, cut up

3 tablespoons Parmesan cheese

1 cup whole milk

1 teaspoon salt

Pinch ground black pepper

4 cups peeled potatoes, thinly sliced

PREHEAT OVEN TO 350°F

In a saucepan, fry bacon until crisp; remove and set aside. Drain all but 1 tablespoon drippings from saucepan. Add onions and green pepper to saucepan; stir and cook until soft. Add cream cheese, Parmesan cheese, milk, salt and black pepper; stir over low heat until cheese is melted. Add potatoes; mix gently. Spoon mixture into a 10x6-inch baking dish. Crumble the crisp bacon over top. Bake 50 to 55 minutes or until potatoes are tender. Serves 6.

Most Minnesotans love potatoes. This side dish is a little like scalloped potatoes...but a little different.

Scalloped Yams Hot Dish

1/4 cup brown sugar, packed

3 tablespoons butter, softened

3 tablespoons all-purpose flour

6 tablespoons finely chopped pecans

6 medium yams peeled, cut into 1/2-inch rounds

1 1/2 cups heavy cream, heated

PREHEAT OVEN TO 375°F

In a bowl, mix sugar, butter and flour until well combined; set aside. Bring a large pot of salted water to a boil. Add yams; cook until crisp-tender, about 5 minutes. Do not overcook. Drain and rinse under cold running water. In a lightly buttered 13x9x2-inch baking dish, arrange yams overlapping in vertical rows. Pour cream over yams. Bake 20 minutes. Crumble pecan mixture over yams, and continue baking until yams are tender and topping is brown, about 25 minutes. Serves 8.

Use sweet potatoes in place of yams if desired.

Spiced Macaroni & Cheese

2 tablespoons butter

3 tablespoons all-purpose flour

2 cups whole milk

1/2 cup picante sauce

3/4 teaspoon ground cumin

1/2 teaspoon salt

2 cups shredded sharp cheddar cheese, divided

1/2 cup chopped green bell pepper

2 cups elbow macaroni, cooked according to package directions, drained

PREHEAT OVEN TO 350°F

In a large saucepan, melt butter over medium heat. Stir in flour until mixture is smooth and bubbly. Remove from heat; gradually stir in milk. Stir in picante sauce, cumin and salt. Bring to a boil over medium heat, stirring constantly until sauce thickens. Stir and cook 1 minute. Remove from heat. Add 1 3/4 cups cheese and green bell pepper; stir until cheese melts. Add cooked macaroni to cheese sauce; mix well. Pour mixture into a 1 1/2-quart baking dish. Top with remaining cheese. Cover and bake 15 minutes. Uncover and bake 5 minutes. Serves 6.

Macaroni and cheese...a comfort food. This side dish adds a little spice.

Spinach Noodle Hot Dish

1 8-ounce package egg noodles

1/2 pound kielbasa sausage, cut into round slices then cut in half

2 cups dairy sour cream

2 tablespoons fresh chives or green onion tops

3/4 teaspoon salt, divided

1 8-ounce package cream cheese, softened

1/2 cup whole milk

1 10-ounce package frozen chopped spinach, thawed, squeezed dry

1/4 teaspoon ground nutmeg

1 cup shredded Swiss cheese

Paprika

PREHEAT OVEN TO 350°F

Cook noodles according to package directions for 7 minutes; drain. Rinse with cold water to cool fast; drain well. In a large bowl, stir together noodles, kielbasa, sour cream, chives and 1/2 teaspoon salt. In another bowl, stir together cream cheese and milk until smooth. Stir in spinach, nutmeg and remaining salt. Spoon half the noodle mixture into a 13x9x2-inch baking dish. Spread cream cheese mixture over noodles. Spoon remaining noodle mixture on top. Cover with foil. Bake 25 minutes. Remove foil. Sprinkle evenly with Swiss cheese. Sprinkle lightly with paprika. Serves 8.

Use other type sausage in this hot dish if desired.

Sweet Potato Apple Hot Dish

6 medium size sweet potatoes, peeled, sliced

1/2 teaspoon ground cinnamon

1/4 teaspoon salt or to taste

4 large apples, peeled, cored, sliced

1/2 cup brown sugar, packed

1 tablespoon fresh lemon juice

1/2 cup butter

3/4 cup pecans, coarsely chopped

PREHEAT OVEN TO 375°F

Layer sweet potatoes in a greased 13x9x2-inch glass baking dish. Sprinkle evenly with cinnamon and salt. Place apples over sweet potatoes. Sprinkle with brown sugar; drizzle evenly with lemon juice. Dot with butter. Sprinkle evenly with pecans. Cover with foil. Bake about 1 hour or until sweet potatoes are done. Serves 8.

Sweet potatoes and apples...a nice combination.

Sweet Potato Bake

2 17-ounce cans sweet potatoes, drained, mashed

1 cup plus 2 tablespoons (10 tablespoons) granulated sugar

2 eggs

1 teaspoon vanilla extract

1/3 cup milk

1/4 cup butter, melted

2/3 cup brown sugar, packed

1/3 cup all-purpose flour

1/3 cup soft butter

1 cup chopped pecans

PREHEAT OVEN TO 350°F

In a bowl, combine sweet potatoes, granulated sugar, eggs, vanilla, milk and melted butter. Beat with an electric mixer until smooth. Spoon mixture into a greased 2-quart baking dish. In another bowl, combine brown sugar, flour, soft butter and pecans. Sprinkle over top of potato mixture. Bake 30 minutes. Serves 8.

This tasty dish can be used as a side dish or dessert when topped with a dollop of whipped cream.

Tofu Potato Hot Dish

2 pounds russet potatoes

1 10½-ounce package soft-pressed silken tofu

1 cup chopped onions

6 cloves garlic, minced

1 tablespoon olive oil

2 tablespoon fresh parsley, chopped

1 teaspoon salt

¼ teaspoon ground black pepper

PREHEAT OVEN TO 350°F

In a large deep saucepan, boil potatoes without peeling until tender. Remove skins. Place potatoes in a food processor. Add tofu; process until smooth. In another saucepan, stir and cook onions and garlic in olive until soft. Add to processor. Add remaining ingredients. Process until blended. Spoon mixture into a greased 2-quart baking dish. Bake 35 minutes or until heated through and is brown on top. Serves 6.

Tofu is gaining popularity in Minnesota...serve this as a side dish or a main dish with favorite steamed fresh vegetables.

Yellow Squash Side Dish

- 2 eggs
- 1 cup cottage cheese
- 1 tablespoon minced yellow onions
- 2 tablespoons all-purpose flour
- 2 teaspoons chicken-flavor instant bouillon granules
- 8 cups sliced yellow crook-neck squash, cooked, drained
- 1 cup shredded sharp cheddar cheese
- 6 slices bacon, cooked crisp, crumbled

PREHEAT OVEN TO 350°F

In a large bowl, combine eggs, cottage cheese, onions, flour and bouillon. Add squash; mix well. Pour mixture into a 11x7x2-inch baking dish. Top with cheddar cheese and bacon. Bake 25 minutes. Let stand 5 minutes before serving. Serves 6.

Yellow squash grows well in my Minnesota garden. This is a good dish to make use of them.

DESSERT DISHES

Almond-Pear Pudding

- 4 firm-ripe pears, peeled, cored, sliced
- 2 tablespoons fresh lemon juice
- 3/4 cup sliced blanched almonds, divided
- 3/4 cup whole milk
- 1/2 cup butter, melted, cooled, divided
- 3 large eggs, lightly beaten
- 3/4 teaspoon pure vanilla extract
- 1/4 teaspoon pure almond extract
- 3/4 cup self-rising flour
- 1 cup plus 2 tablespoons (10 table-spoons) granulated sugar, divided
- 1/4 teaspoon salt

PREHEAT OVEN TO 400°F

In a buttered 10x2-inch round glass baking dish (1 quart), toss pears with lemon juice; arrange evenly in dish. In a blender, add 1/2 cup almonds; grind fine. Add milk, 6 tablespoons melted butter, eggs, vanilla and almond extract; blend mixture until smooth. In a bowl, combine flour 1/2 cup sugar and salt; add to milk mixture, stirring until combined. Pour batter over pears. Drizzle with remaining butter, and sprinkle with remaining sugar and almonds. Bake in the middle of oven 40 minutes, and is golden brown. Cool 15 minutes before serving. Serves 6.

Serve this delicious pudding with sweetened whipped cream or vanilla ice cream as desired.

Apple Betty Bake

3 cups peeled, sliced apples

1½ cups soft white bread crumbs, divided

6 tablespoons brown sugar

1 teaspoon ground cinnamon

5 tablespoons butter, melted, divided

¾ cup hot water mixed with teaspoon vanilla extract

Whipped cream

Vanilla ice cream

PREHEAT OVEN TO 350°F

In a bowl, combine apples, 1 cup bread crumbs, sugar and cinnamon. Place into a buttered 1½-quart baking dish. In a saucepan, combine 4 tablespoons melted butter and water; pour on top apple mixture. In a bowl, combine remaining bread crumbs and remaining melted butter; sprinkle evenly on top. Bake about 35 to 40 minutes. Serve warm with whipped cream or vanilla ice cream. Serves 6.

Apple Betty dates back to the '50s...delicious.

Berries 'n Peach Crumble

1¼ cups granulated sugar, divided

3 tablespoons cornstarch

½ cup cold water

1 teaspoon vanilla extract

1 16-ounce package frozen sliced peaches, thawed

1 cup cranberries, fresh or frozen

1 cup all-purpose flour

½ teaspoon baking powder

Pinch salt

½ cup butter, melted

¼ cup whole milk

PREHEAT OVEN TO 400°F

In a large saucepan, combine 1 cup sugar and cornstarch. Gradually stir in water until well blended; bring to a boil, stirring constantly. Stir and cook until thickened, about 1 minute. Stir in fruit; bring to a boil, stirring often. Remove from heat. Stir in vanilla. Pour mixture into an ungreased 8-inch square glass baking dish. In a bowl, combine flour, remaining sugar, baking powder and salt; mix well. Stir in butter and milk; mix well. Drop mixture by spoonfuls over hot fruit mixture. Bake 25 minutes. Remove from oven; let stand 10 minutes before serving. Serves 8.

A great dessert hot dish for afternoon tea.

BJ's Raspberry Apple Crisp

- 5 cups Granny green apples, peeled cored, sliced
- 1 pint fresh raspberries
- 1 teaspoon vanilla extract
- 1/2 cup packed brown sugar
- 1/2 cup granulated sugar
- 1 teaspoon ground cinnamon
- 3/4 cup all-purpose flour
- 8 tablespoons cold butter
- Peanut brittle, crushed
- Vanilla ice cream
- Whipped cream

PREHEAT OVEN TO 350°F

Layer apples on bottom of a well-buttered shallow 2½-quart baking dish. Place a layer of raspberries over apples. Drizzle evenly with vanilla extract. In a bowl, combine sugars, cinnamon and flour. Add butter; cut in with a pastry blender until crumbly; sprinkle evenly over raspberries. Sprinkle enough peanut brittle to cover last layer. Bake about 35 to 40 minutes or until apples are soft. Serve warm topped with vanilla ice cream or whipped cream. Serves 8.

Other apples may be used in this sweet crisp.

Blueberry Bread Pudding

- ³/₄ cup heavy cream, divided
- ³/₄ cup half & half (light cream)
- ¹/₄ cup pure maple syrup
- ³/₄ teaspoon pure vanilla extract
- 2 large eggs
- 4 cups French bread cubes
- 1 cup fresh or frozen blueberries
- ¹/₄ teaspoon freshly grated lemon peel
- 2 tablespoons powdered sugar
- 1¹/₄ tablespoons fresh lemon juice

PREHEAT OVEN TO 350°F

In a medium bowl, whisk together ¹/₄ cup heavy cream, half & half, maple syrup, vanilla and eggs; pour mixture over bread cubes in a large bowl, mixing well. Fold in blue berries. Pour mixture into a 2-quart glass baking dish. Refrigerate 15 minutes. Bake uncovered until set, about 35 minutes. In a medium bowl, using an electric mixer at medium speed, beat remaining ¹/₂ cup heavy cream. When slightly thickened, add lemon peel and powdered sugar. Slowly add lemon juice; whip until stiff. Refrigerate. Serve bread pudding warm with lemon-whipped cream as desired. Serves 4.

For best flavor, use pure maple syrup only.

Busy Day Cherry Cobbler

2 21-ounce cans cherry pie filling

1 teaspoon lemon juice

1/2 teaspoon vanilla extract

1 1/2 cups all-purpose flour

5 tablespoon granulated sugar, divided

1 teaspoon baking powder

1/2 teaspoon salt

5 1/2 tablespoons butter, chilled

3 tablespoons whole milk

1 egg, slightly beaten

Sweetened whipped cream

Vanilla ice cream

PREHEAT OVEN TO 350°F

In a large bowl, combine pie filling, lemon juice and vanilla until well blended. Pour mixture into an ungreased 13x9x2-inch glass baking dish. In a medium bowl, combine flour 2 tablespoons sugar, baking powder and salt. With a pastry blender or 2 knives, cut in butter until crumbly. With a fork, stir in milk and egg just until moistened. Spoon mixture over filling in baking dish; sprinkle with remaining sugar. Bake 40 to 45 minutes or until golden brown and bubbly around edges. Serve warm with whipped cream or ice cream. Serves 8 to 10.

Substitute your favorite fruit pie filling...if apple is used, add a little ground cinnamon with the sugar.

Chocolate Bread Pudding

- 2 1-ounce squares semi-sweet chocolate
- 3 cups whole milk
- 1/4 teaspoon salt
- 1/2 cup brown sugar, packed
- 2 eggs, separated
- 1 1/2 teaspoons vanilla extract
- 6 slices dry white bread, cut into 1/2-inch cubes
- 4 tablespoons granulated sugar
- 2 tablespoons shaved semi-sweet chocolate

PREHEAT OVEN TO 350°F

In a double boiler, heat 2-ounces chocolate and milk until chocolate is melted. Add salt. In a bowl, whisk brown sugar and egg yolks until combined; gradually add chocolate mixture stirring constantly. Stir in vanilla. Combine bread and chocolate mixture in a bowl; let stand 15 minutes, stirring occasionally. Spoon into a buttered 2-quart baking dish. Place dish in a pan of hot water; bake 30 minutes or until almost firm. Beat egg whites until foamy; add half of granulated sugar, beating until blended. Add remaining granulated sugar; continue beating until mixture will stand in peaks. Pile meringue lightly into mounds in a border around edge of pudding. Sprinkle meringue with shaved chocolate, and continue baking 8 minutes or until meringue is light brown. Serves 6.

When serving, top with whipped cream if desired.

Coconut Bread Pudding

1 1-pound loaf white bread, cut into 1-inch cubes, divided

1/2 cup dried apricots, cut into thin strips, divided

1/2 cup shredded coconut, divided

2 15-ounce cans cream of coconut

2 cups whole milk

1 tablespoon vanilla extract

1 1/2 cups granulated sugar

6 eggs

Vanilla ice cream

Whipped cream

Powdered sugar

Toasted coconut

PREHEAT OVEN TO 350°F

Line bottom of a 10x12x3-inch baking dish with half the bread cubes; sprinkle half the apricots and half the coconut over top. Repeat layer. In a saucepan, heat milk, cream of coconut, vanilla and sugar until sugar is completely dissolved and milk is warm but not hot, stirring occasionally. Remove from heat. In another bowl, beat eggs, and slowly stir in 1 cup warm milk mixture, then slowly stir into first milk mixture until well blended. Ladle mixture over bread. Cover with foil, and place dish in a pan filled with hot water half way up sides of pan. Bake 1 hour. Remove foil; bake 10 minutes. Remove dish from water bath. Serve with the last four ingredients as desired. Serves 10.

The Rainforest Cafe in the Mall of America serves this bread pudding...a good reason to stop in!

Favorite Peach Cobbler

- 1/4 cup butter, melted
- 1 cup all-purpose flour
- 1 cup granulated sugar
-   Pinch salt
- 1 tablespoon baking powder
- 1 16-ounce can sliced peaches in heavy syrup, undrained
- 3/4 cup whole milk
- 1 1/4 teaspoons vanilla extract
- 1/4 teaspoon ground nutmeg
- 1/4 rounded teaspoon ground cinnamon
-   Half of 1 fresh lemon
-   Vanilla ice cream

PREHEAT OVEN TO 350°F

Place butter in an 11x7x2-inch shallow glass baking dish. In a bowl, sift together flour, sugar, salt and baking powder. Add milk; stir well. Pour mixture into prepared baking dish–Do Not Stir. Top evenly with peaches and juice, cutting a few peaches in half–Do Not Stir. Drizzle evenly with vanilla. Sprinkle evenly with nutmeg and cinnamon. Squeeze the half lemon evenly over top–Do Not Stir. Bake 40 minutes or until golden brown. Serve warm with vanilla ice cream. Serves 8.

This cobbler is delicious and easy to prepare. I serve it often to company...most ask for the recipe.

Fresh Fruit Cranberry Crisp

3 cups sliced, peeled fresh apples

2 cups sliced, peeled fresh pears

1½ cups fresh cranberries

1 cup granulated sugar

1 teaspoon vanilla extract

7½ tablespoons all-purpose flour, divided

¾ teaspoon ground cinnamon

1 cup quick oatmeal, uncooked

½ cup brown sugar, packed

¼ cup butter

¼ cup chopped walnuts

Sweetened whipped cream

PREHEAT OVEN TO 375°F

In a large bowl, toss together fruits, granulated sugar, vanilla, 2 tablespoons flour and cinnamon. Spoon mixture evenly into a buttered 2-quart shallow baking dish. In another bowl, combine oat meal, brown sugar and remaining flour; mix well. Add butter, cutting in with a pastry blender until crumbly. Add nuts; mix well. Sprinkle mixture over fruit. Bake about 40 minutes or until apples are tender and top is golden brown. Serve with whipped cream as desired. Serves 8.

Use frozen cranberries when fresh are not available.

Fresh Pineapple Cobbler

1³/4 cups granulated sugar, divided

6 tablespoons biscuit baking mix, mixed with 1 teaspoon freshly grated lemon peel

4 cups fresh pineapple chunks

1 teaspoon vanilla extract

³/4 cup biscuit baking mix

1 large egg, beaten

1/4 cup butter, melted

Vanilla ice cream

PREHEAT OVEN TO 350°F

In a bowl, combine 1 cup sugar, 6 tablespoons biscuit mix with lemon peel. Add pineapple and vanilla; mix well. Spoon mixture into a buttered 9-inch square baking dish. In another bowl, combine ³/4 cup biscuit mix, remaining sugar and egg. Sprinkle over top. Drizzle evenly with melted butter. Bake about 45 minutes or until golden brown. Serve warm, topped with vanilla ice cream. Serves 8.

Top with a dollop of whipped cream if desired.

Gingered Rhubarb Crisp

1 cup oatmeal, uncooked

1 cup brown sugar

1/2 cup all-purpose flour

1/2 teaspoon salt

8 tablespoons cold butter

4 cups diced fresh or frozen rhubarb

2 tablespoons chopped candied ginger

1/2 cup granulated sugar

Vanilla ice cream

PREHEAT OVEN TO 350°F

In a bowl, combine oatmeal, brown sugar, flour and salt. Add butter; cut in with a pastry blender until crumbly. Spread half the mixture onto bottom of a greased 8-inch square baking dish; press gently to form crust. Cover crust with rhubarb; sprinkle with ginger and granulated sugar. Top with remaining oatmeal mixture. Bake about 45 minutes or until rhubarb is tender and top is brown. Serve warm, topped with vanilla ice cream as desired. Serves 8.

Most Minnesotans have a rhubarb plant growing in the garden or in a flower bed...great stuff.

Mary Dow's Bread Pudding

1 8-ounce loaf French bread, thinly sliced

1/4 cup golden raisins

3 tablespoons butter, melted

6 large eggs

3/4 granulated sugar

3 cups whole cold milk

1/2 teaspoon ground cinnamon

1 tablespoon vanilla extract

Sauce:

3 large egg yolks

6 tablespoons granulated sugar

2 cups hot whole milk

1 tablespoon bourbon, optional

1 teaspoon vanilla extract

PREHEAT OVEN TO 350°F

In a bowl, combine bread, raisins and butter. In another bowl, whisk 6 eggs and 3/4 cup sugar. Whisk in 3 cups cold milk, cinnamon and 1 tablespoon vanilla. Pour mixture over bread; let stand 30 minutes. Spoon mixture into a greased 11x7x2-inch baking dish. Place dish into a pan filled with water half way up sides of pan. Bake 1 hour or until set in center. Remove dish from water bath. Using an electric mixer, beat egg yolks and 6 tablespoons sugar in a bowl, until thick and forms a ribbon when beaters are lifted. Gradually beat in hot milk; pour mixture into a saucepan. Stir and cook about 8 minutes, until sauce coats back of a metal spoon. Cool. Stir in bourbon and 1 teaspoon vanilla. Serve pudding warm, topped with sauce. Serves 8.

For best texture, do not remove crusts from bread.

Raspberry Bread Pudding

8 slices day-old French bread, crusts removed, cubed

1 tablespoon butter, melted

1 cup fresh raspberries, cleaned

1 cup half & half (light cream)

2 large eggs, slightly beaten

1 teaspoon vanilla extract

1/2 cup granulated sugar

Sweetened whipped cream

PREHEAT OVEN TO 350°F

Toss bread with melted butter until coated; place into a 1-quart buttered baking dish. Sprinkle evenly with raspberries. In a bowl, whisk half & half, eggs, vanilla and sugar until blended. Pour over raspberries. Cover and place baking dish in a pan of hot water reaching half way up sides of pan. Bake 45 minutes or until set. Remove dish from water bath. Serve topped with whipped cream as desired. Serves 4.

Garnish with additional fresh raspberries when serving, if desired.

Spiced Banana Bread Pudding

- 4 cups day-old French bread, cubed into 1-inch pieces
- 7 tablespoons butter, melted, divided
- 3 large eggs, lightly beaten
- 2 cups whole milk
- 1 cup plus 2 tablespoons (10 tablespoons) granulated sugar, divided
- 1 tablespoon pure vanilla extract, divided
- 1/2 teaspoon ground cinnamon
- 1/2 teaspoon ground nutmeg
- 1/4 teaspoon salt
- 1 cup ripe-firm bananas, cut into 1/4-inch pieces
- 1 tablespoon cornstarch
- 3/4 cup light cream
- 2 teaspoons light corn syrup

PREHEAT OVEN TO 375°F

In a 2-quart buttered baking dish, toss bread and 4 tablespoons melted butter until coated. In a bowl, combine eggs, 8 tablespoons sugar, 2 teaspoons vanilla, cinnamon, nutmeg and salt; mix well. Add bananas; mix well. Pour mixture over bread; stir until coated. Bake uncovered about 40 minutes or until a knife inserted near center comes out clean. In a saucepan, add remaining butter. In a bowl, combine remaining sugar and cornstarch; stir into butter. Add cream and corn syrup; stir and cook over medium heat until mixture comes to a boil. Boil 1 minute. Remove from heat; stir in remaining vanilla. Serve pudding warm topped with warm sauce. Serves 6.

When serving, top with whipped cream if desired.

Tasty Cherry Crunch

2 cups all-purpose flour

1 cup quick-cooking oatmeal, uncooked

1 cup corn flakes

1/4 cup flaked coconut

2 tablespoons chopped almonds

1 cup brown sugar, packed

3/4 teaspoon baking soda

Pinch salt

3/4 cup butter, melted

1 teaspoon vanilla extract

2 21-ounce cans cherry pie filling

Vanilla ice cream

PREHEAT OVEN TO 350°F

In a bowl, combine flour, oatmeal, cornflakes, flaked coconut, almonds, brown sugar, baking soda and salt. Add butter and vanilla extract. Mix together until crumbly, using a pastry blender. Reserve half the crumbly mixture. Spoon remaining crumbly mixture into a 13x9x2-inch baking dish; pat down evenly. Spread cherry filling evenly over crust. Sprinkle top evenly with reserved crumb mixture. Bake 45 minutes. Serve warm with vanilla ice cream. Serves 12.

This is an easy cherry dessert to prepare.

Trader's Rhubarb Crisp

1 cup all-purpose flour
3/4 cup oatmeal, uncooked
1 cup brown sugar
   Pinch salt
1 teaspoon ground cinnamon
1/2 cup butter, melted
4 cups diced or sliced rhubarb
1 cup granulated sugar
2 tablespoons cornstarch
1 cup water
1 teaspoon pure vanilla extract
   Vanilla ice cream

PREHEAT OVEN TO 350°F

In a bowl, combine flour, oatmeal, brown sugar, salt and cinnamon; mix well. Stir in butter. Place half the mixture into a buttered 9x9-inch square baking dish. Top with rhubarb. In a saucepan, combine granulated sugar and cornstarch. Stir in water and vanilla. Stir and cook until thick and clear. Pour mixture over rhubarb. Top with remaining flour mixture. Bake 1 hour (will be bubbly). Serve warm topped with ice cream as desired. Serves 12.

Rhubarb is one of my favorite foods...I love it in pies, cakes and warm homemade muffins.

INDEX

About the Author

Theresa Millang is the author of several other cookbooks, including *The Best of Cajun-Creole Recipes*, indicating her versatility as a cook and author. Born in Louisiana and moved to Minnesota via marriage, she adapted quite well to "hot dish country" and brought her creative kitchen skills to the task.